Employee-Centered Management

The Coming Revolution in Social Services

First Edition

by
Larry Wenger

January, 2014

Newtown, Pennsylvania
U.S.A.

**With Forward by William Waldman,
CSWM, Executive-in-Residence
Rutgers University School of Social Work**

ISBN: 1493623729
ISBN 13: 9781493623723
Library of Congress Control Number: 2013920588
CreateSpace Independent Publishing Platform
North Charleston, South Carolina

About Larry Wenger

Larry is a graduate of the University of Kansas School of Social Work. Over the years he has held a variety of leadership positions in social services. He has led organizations providing child welfare services, programs for persons with disabilities, organizations providing behavioral health services as well as juvenile justice and corrections.

Until 2005, Larry was Associate Executive Director of Catholic Charities, Diocese of Metuchen, a $50 million organization with a variety of social service programs operating over four counties in central NJ. Prior to that he was Director of Program Development for Covenant House in New York where he coordinated efforts to establish programs for runaway and homeless youth in Houston, Ft. Lauderdale, New Orleans, Boston and Guatemala.

In 2005 he started Foundations for Community Programs, Inc., doing business as Workforce Performance Group. Since then he has been involved in training front line social service supervisors and managers, helping them to better understand their responsibility as leaders. Hundreds of persons have participated in Larry's leadership workshops. A particular focus has been on helping agencies to become places of challenge, growth and high levels of satisfaction for employees.

Larry lives in Newtown, Pa with his wife Diane and daughter Kristi. He has two other children and four grandchildren. He is an avid builder and sailor of boats and a licensed amateur radio operator. He is active in the community as: a member of the Board of Directors for the Wordsworth Academy of Philadelphia, Pa;. the Lower Bucks Chamber of Commerce; the Suburban Networking Group and serves as chairman of the Administrative Council of the Trinity United Methodist Church of Ewing, NJ.

Personal Message from the Author

Thank you so much for your interest in this book. I hope that you find it to be helpful to you and your organization. What I really enjoy is hearing from my readers. So if you have thoughts or questions you would like to share with me about this book, I would love to receive your email at lwenger@workforceperformancegroup.net.

In the near future, I hope to sponsor a series of free, interactive webcasts – just for people who are interested in this book and want to discuss it with me, and other readers, face-to-face.

To receive our free, weekly, management news/opinion letter send an email to the above address and type "Sign Me Up" in the Subject line. Among other things, that is where we will announce the schedule for our webcases.

Definition

"Employee Centered Management is a unique approach to allocating resources and guiding day to day organizational decisions. Employee-Centered Management places priority on the needs of and interests of employees. Leaders who judiciously use this approach believe that by doing so the organization actually provides superior service to customers, clients and consumers of service."
-Larry Wenger, MSW

Forward

By William Waldman, CSWM

In *Employee Centered Management: The Coming Revolution in Social Services,* Larry Wenger has produced an extraordinarily valuable text, guide, and primer for those who have, or aspire to have, leadership roles in social service organizations. The last quarter century has produced truly momentous changes and challenges for those organizations and has driven an almost Darwinian evolution in which those unable to adapt have or will fail. There is no question that this change will progress at a geometric rate in the quarter century to come and beyond.

Changes in public policy including the privatization of vast swaths of the human services from government to the private sector, new methods of contracting for services, a turbulent economy that has diminished governmental and philanthropic sources of support, profound changes in the workforce, a demand for greater accountability for outcomes; and, vastly expanding applications of information technology are all a part of the shifting landscape. Social service organizations now attempt to position themselves to survive and thrive by strategically analyzing new corporate options including mergers, acquisitions, social entrepreneurship and joint ventures with other such organizations.

Given the fact that the social services are among the most labor intensive of industries, the author correctly focuses on perhaps the greatest and most central challenge of all – recruiting, supporting, growing and retaining the workforce necessary for a social services organization to achieve its mission and vision. Absent a vital, diverse and ever up-skilling workforce with the necessary competencies, the other challenges will never be met.

This book compresses the vast experience and learning of the author, recognized best practices and evidence based theory into twenty strategies for human resource or talent management in an eminently readable fashion. His examples from his own experiences and those of others are woven into "teachable moments" which enliven and elucidate the critical points he makes. The discussion questions listed at the end of each strategy facilitate both learning and teaching making this a useful text for an academic setting as well. This work deeply resonates with my own experience of leading large public and private organizations from a management or governance standpoint for the past four decades and I believe that like me, you will both learn from and enjoy this book.

William Waldman, MSW, CSWM
Lecturer and Executive in Residence
Rutgers University School of Social Work
New Brunswick, New Jersey

Biographical Sketch of

William Waldman, CSWM

Title: Lecturer and Executive in Residence, Rutgers University
School of Social Work

Education: Pennsylvania State University, University Park, PA.,
BA Degree, 1965 – English; Rutgers – The State
University of New Jersey – School of Social Work, New
Brunswick, NJ, MSW Degree, 1972, Administration,
Policy and Planning.

Professional Experience

Mr. Waldman has served as a Visiting Professor and Lecturer and
Executive in Residence at the Rutgers University School of Social
Work since January, 2001. From July 1998 to December, 2000
he was the Executive Director of the American Public Human
Services Association (APHSA) in Washington, DC. APHSA is a
non-profit organization whose members include the health and
human service agencies in the 50 states, as well as many agencies
in counties, municipalities and US territories. Its purpose is to
develop, promote and assist its members in the implementation
of sound public human services policies.

Mr. Waldman was employed by the State of New Jersey from
July 1987 to June 1998 during which time he served as a Director of
the Division of Youth and Family Services – the state's child welfare
agency, as Deputy Commissioner of the New Jersey Department

of Human Services and as Commissioner of the Department and a member of the cabinet for three Governors of New Jersey.

The Department of Human Services is the largest public agency in New Jersey and his responsibilities included administering a $7 billion budget, managing a workforce of 19,000 employees and serving over one million residents of the state. The Department encompassed seven (7) operating divisions which included the Medicaid program, services to the mentally ill and developmentally disabled, the child welfare program, all public welfare programs as well as services to the blind and visually impaired and the deaf and hard of hearing. He also had responsibility for eighteen (18) institutions including psychiatric hospitals, developmental centers, children's residential facilities and a residential program for the blind.

From May of 1975 until July of 1987 Mr. Waldman directed the Middlesex County, New Jersey Department of Human Services. In this capacity he was responsible for the administration of numerous county- based human services programs, managed a staff of sixty-five (65) employees, and administered a budget in the amount of $8 million.

Mr. Waldman was employed from October of 1965 to May of 1975 with the Essex County Welfare Board in Newark, New Jersey. He began as a caseworker and advanced through a series of progressively responsible supervisory and administrative positions including the administration of the County's food stamp and employment and training programs.

Mr. Waldman has been the recipient of numerous awards throughout his career, serves on various boards of directors of community agencies, has made numerous presentations at professional conferences, the New Jersey Legislature, the US Congress, foundations and business and industry groups; and, consulted for both government and private agencies.

Table of Contents

Introduction

Happy Employees = Happy Clients

"Good bosses care about getting important things done.
Exceptional bosses care about their people too."
- Jeff Haden

I decided to write this book because I have seen too many examples where social service leaders have been disrespectful to hardworking, competent and dedicated employees. I am convinced however that this can and will change over the coming years.

This book is about that coming change and what it will look like. The change will mean that agency resources will be directed toward helping employees feel more satisfied and engaged with their work. The needs of employees will have higher priority in the management of agency resources. There are three contributing factors which will bring about this revolution:

1. Leadership at the top of the agency is changing, and the status quo momentum which some of them represent will no longer be there. This is a simple demographic factor in that nearly 70% of social services executives will reach the age of retirement by the year 2020.
2. Later, I will illustrate the many progressive "people management" practices have been developed and successfully

implemented in the for-profit community. Eventually these practices will filter their way into the non-profit world. The result of this innovation in the for-profit community is that when employees are taken care of, the company's bottom line improves.

3. The nature of the workforce is changing. Today's generation of workers want to be involved in the development of the organization; they want to be part of a cause. They are not content to just respond to direction that comes down from above. They are looking for the kind of transparency that makes it easy and encourages them to be involved in the agency's long range planning. They have grown up with technology and they expect that their workplace will fully utilize available technological resources. Most importantly, they want a different quality of life than did their peers a generation earlier; they want work to be blended with family. Typically they are not prepared to give up a personal, family life for the benefit of the agency or its clients.

I was recently struck by a social media post written by a social worker who said that she was tired of being "belittled and dehumanized" by her supervisor. The response to this post was almost viral. In the next several days more than 200 people responded to her, some to offer solace and suggestion, others to say, often dejectedly, "I've had the same experience." There are a lot of dissatisfied social workers.

But it's not only social workers who are dissatisfied. The 2013 Gallup Engagement Survey found that only 30% of American workers are fully engaged in their work. They conclude that this lack of engagement costs American businesses $540 billion each year. Sadly, my conclusion is that social service organizations are absorbing their share of this loss. In human service organizations, helping staff grow and develop ought to come naturally but this is not **always** the case.

Much has been written about the problems of and challenges to social agencies in the 21st Century. These issues are discussed in social media as well as the <u>Harvard Business Review</u> and the <u>Chronicle of Philanthropy.</u> Among other citations this material describes leaders who lack the needed vision and willingness to risk; the short-sightedness of living from one grant to another and the lack of leaders who know how to lead.

These are important issues. At a more basic level however, I have seen extensive examples of daily operational decisions or stalemates which frustrate employees, contribute to burnout, high turnover, poor morale and mediocre service. For example I have seen agencies where employees have not had a one-on-one meeting with their supervisor in two years. Or where the janitorial staff does not regularly clean the restrooms and no one does anything about it. Or where new employees receive no orientation or formal introduction to the agency. Leaders must take seriously their "obligation to remain relevant to the employee and not the other way around."

And so, this book is my attempt to describe 20 strategies that will happen in social services. I believe that in the future these strategies will be utilized in thriving and healthy social service organizations. These are the features that will enable employees to be excited about coming to work and will make it possible for them to brag to others about their on-the-job accomplishments. I do not talk about clinical services and I do not talk about paying people more money, although both are important. This is about the employee experience of working for an agency. These are strategies for making one's workplace not only successful, but an exciting place to be. Engaged employees contribute value to the organization; that is, they are worth more than they are paid. Will they hop out of bed *every morning*, ready to solve all world's problems? Probably not. But more days than not, they will find a lot of satisfaction in their work.

It is worth noting here that this is not a book about what organizations can do to make employees happy. Their happiness is after all, in large measure their own responsibility. Happiness and employee motivation however are highly related concepts. It is the responsibility of employers to create a workplace environment which encourages employee growth, success, excitement and engagement or motivation. However, even though employers successfully create these conditions, it is the employee who decides to develop the internal motivation which leads to a feeling of happiness about the job situation.

I believe that in order for organizations to do a good job of providing service, they must start by learning how to take care of employees. It's been said for years that "employees are our most important asset." But often we treat them as a distinct liability to be eliminated at the first sign of trouble. Their need to grow and change seems neglected. The importance of their families and personal lives is rarely blended with the demands of the workplace. Their suggestions are generally ignored or discouraged. *Most importantly there is little commitment to the idea that in order to do a good job helping people, employees need to be happily engaged in their work*

There are some strikingly successful models of employee engagement in the for-profit corporate world. Southwest Airlines for example, the nation's most profitable airline, believes that when employees are happy, customers will follow. The Pike Place Fish Market in Seattle, has taught low wage workers how to have fun on the job and has watched its sales soar along with the general economic climate of Seattle's once-crumbling waterfront. Tony Hsieh, CEO of Zappos says that "wow" customer service begins with engaged employees.

Social service organizations have often followed management innovation in the for-profit sector by 5 or 10 years. It is now time for not-for-profit agencies to prepare for change.

A new approach and formula is needed to ensure the future of our organizations, and must include a greater investment in the happiness and engagement of our employees.

Social service organizations have generally thought that all available resources should go to the needs of the individuals served. The new formula and approach asks you to look at it differently. The command and control management approach is outdated and what is needed is an approach to management which is built around positive employee-supervisor relationships. The times are changing and the old style of management needs to change in kind.

Change is needed so organizations can see the potential of employees to be the *main* drivers of success. In the course of this book's 20 chapters, I will discuss the concrete steps that organizations can and should be taking in order to maximize the value of employees. Each chapter is followed by a series of discussion questions in the hope that they enable leaders to interact with their employees on these important topics. Some topics are very interrelated. Therefore some themes are repeated which only speaks to the connection and the importance of the idea, namely increasing employee value.

I do not necessarily have the final answer on some of these difficult questions. Some of my recommendations may not sound right to you. You may find yourself in strong disagreement. When that happens and you can find an even better answer for your organization, I will have met my goal.

One final note. If you want to implement some of these strategies, or perhaps you already are implementing them, be clear about what you are trying to accomplish. Relate your changes and innovations to the needs of the organization. If you hope that training can reduce employee turnover, as it often does, make sure you measure turnover, before, during and after training. Measure the success of your implementation with a data-based measurement of outcomes.

Thank you for your interest in this important topic and I wish you all the best.

Larry Wenger, MSW
Newtown, Pa.

one

Hire the Right People in the First Place

**"When I'm hiring a cook for one of my
restaurants, and I want to see what they can do,
I usually ask them to make me an omelet."**
- Bobby Flay

The Problem

Sometimes, those of us who lead non-profit organizations
are inclined to hire anyone with a normal temperature. We
make the assumption that anyone willing to work for subsistence
wages is qualified to do what we need them to do. We point with
pride to the hard work being done by underpaid staff members,
as well we should. But it all comes back to bite us when those
semi-volunteers leave us after three months to pursue their next
dream. Or the mismatch can be so great that it leaves a new hire
with little choice but to not return from lunch during their first
day on the job.

As most of you know, at non-profits, it is not unusual to see
entry level staff turnover in the range of 30-50% and turnover
rates above that are not unheard of by any means. All of this
leads to excessive personnel costs and dissatisfaction amongst
the people we are trying to help; no one likes a constant parade
of people in and out of their lives.

"His interview was great but after he started the job, he turned out to be my worst nightmare." Sound familiar? Jack Welch, once a popular leadership guru when he was in charge of General Electric said that there are three kinds of employees: Builders, Cutters and Maintainers. <u>Builders</u> are self-motivated from day one. They need very little supervision to get started. They motivate others, and generally make good decisions. When you give them something to do, you can count on them accomplishing that objective and exactly as you had prescribed. They quickly become the "go to" person on your staff. <u>Cutters</u> are staff you never should have hired in the first place. Even the best supervisor will be frustrated in their attempts to motivate them or develop them into consistent performers at any task. They are not stupid, but for whatever reason they under perform, regardless of the challenge level. They make poor decisions and they pay very little attention to the normal expectations of the job. <u>Maintainers</u> will be the ones who do most of your work for you. They come to your job without a lot of creativity or motivation. But they will perform adequately; they will do what they are asked to do, to the best of their ability. Their work is usually accurate, without mistakes.

It only stands to reason that a good supervisor can expand the capability and commitment of Maintainers. At the same time, without supervision or with a bad supervisor their work can easily become unacceptable; some Maintainers will become Cutters under these circumstances. But these are the staff where efforts made to ensure that they have good supervision will have a tremendous payoff. Building your policies, procedures and management approach around the needs of Maintainers, the largest group of staff will have better outcomes for an organization, than the usual approach of building policies around Cutters, or those most likely to cause disruption.

How do we know whether the job applicant, seated in front of us is a builder, cutter or maintainer? Interviewing is the most widely used selection tool, but is often an unreliable method. Why is traditional interviewing unreliable as a predictor of job success? What can you do to make sure your interview will help you determine whether or not an applicant should be hired? Here are some challenges that we typically confront when we are interviewing job candidates.

1. We don't really know what we are looking for. The job description is often out of date and unrealistic so that it is not a good guide for discussion with the applicant. This opens the door for applicants to mislead the interviewer and talk about him or herself in a positive way but one that is not related to the job you want to fill.

2. Most estimates are that as many as 70% of all resumes are seriously embellished. So resumes also are not good discussion guides for the interview.

3. Applicants can make an initially positive impression or a negative impression. Neither may accurately reflect the applicant's true capacity but you spend the rest of the interview looking for responses that justify your initial impression, be it positive or negative. As a result, the interview ends with you really not understanding the applicant comprehensively. In the HR literature this is known as the Halo-Horn Effect.

4. We like to hire applicants where the "chemistry is right." People may be great conversationalists and they may like the same things as we do, like sports, or grandchildren or gardening. But during the hiring phase we are looking for success characteristics, not personal interests.

5. We ask too many "canned" questions like, "What are your strengths or weaknesses?" Remember we live in an internet age where applicants can find stock answers to frequently asked questions with just a mouse click.

6. We compare applicants to each other rather than with the competencies required to do the job successfully. Clearly

stated, required competencies should really be your measuring stick of likely applicant success.

7. We like people who are just like us. They have the same temperament, the same management style, the same likes and dislikes. We feel comfortable around them. But maybe the organization could benefit from someone who is different from us; someone who will ask the tough, uncomfortable questions.

8. Applicants who look good and dress well are impressive. Is looking good and dressing well a likely indicator of on the job success in the position you are trying to fill? An attractive physical appearance is often assumed to be associated with competence and it leads many hiring managers to reach a conclusion about an applicant within a few minutes. Physical appearance may or may not have anything to do with an applicant's competence for the job and worst case, could end you in court around what could appear to be a discriminatory hiring practice.

9. We think we are a good judge of character, but hiring based on your gut feeling is like target shooting in the dark; sometimes you will hit the target but the percentage of misses will be high. Hiring based on a "gut feeling" is a cover-up for the real problem which is that you don't really have any other reason to hire the applicant.

10. We ask "what would you do" questions. Rather, ask "what have you done?" Pose questions that contain a challenge and ask the candidate to describe how he/she has handled a similar situation in the past, either on the job or in their personal life. Remember, past behavior is the best predictor of future behavior.

11. We make a hire decision based on the urgency of filling the vacancy. This often happens especially in situations where staffing levels are contractually required. But it is always a mistake to hire someone just because they are

"available tomorrow." Hire because they satisfactorily meet pre-determined characteristics for job success.

12. We ignore or overlook the following "red flags" –
    a. Negative or vague reasons for leaving past employment
    b. They are unable to clearly describe why they want the job
    c. Job hopping – too many jobs in too little time. Chances are you will be their next 'previous' employer
    d. Poor personal hygiene
    e. Arriving late for the interview or failing to appear without an explanatory phone call

The Solution

How can we do a better job of selecting the right applicant to fill the job opening we have? Several years ago, I realized that I was hearing about a growing divide between HR staff and program staff. Each was blaming the other for the fact that most, if not all, of the staff who were hired, were gone within a year; often within six months. This continual churn of staff was expensive, led to dissatisfied clients, demoralized staff and lots of operational errors.

So I began a search for an intervention that might be helpful. My bias was that the problem of employee turnover could be managed; it was not something to be simply tolerated as a "cost of doing business." This search led me down several dead ends, but I eventually learned about the work of Carol Quinn who had her own version of "motivational interviewing."

What Carol had developed is not the same as the field of motivational interviewing which is part of a clinical process. For Carol, now an internationally known expert on how to hire high performers, *motivational interviewing is a framework for selecting staff who have the skills, passion and attitude for the job.* Motivational Interviewing is truly a "best practice" when it comes to consistently hiring staff who are high performers. Is it foolproof? No, it is not. Is it a significant improvement over hiring based on what our "gut" tells us about an applicant? Absolutely.

Let's take a minute to better understand three important characteristics which Carol has identified as being closely linked to on-the job success.

1. Attitude. What we are looking for in applicants is a "can-do attitude". The determination to solve a problem which may at first seem overwhelming. Frequently, when people do not have this "can-do attitude" they are very prone to blaming their failures on someone else rather than accepting personal responsibility. A recent article in *Business Management Daily,* quoted a Leadership IQ study which found that 46% of new hires are either fired or disciplined within 18 months. And in 89% of those cases, the reason for the action was not incompetence, but attitude. I'll bet most of your "fires" had attitude problems too.

2. Passion. When we talk to employees in group homes and other places where they are caring for vulnerable people, they unanimously agree that to be successful in these jobs, applicants must have "heart" or passion for the job. It means they genuinely like the work and care about their outcomes. And by the way, someone can be skilled at doing the work and not have the necessary passion for the job; these folks are gone soon, looking for greener pastures.

3. Skills. This is the *what* of the job...the often mechanical tasks which must be completed routinely. Remember this. In contrast to attitude and passion, skills can normally be taught. So, here is a place you can sometimes compromise: if someone has the can-do attitude and a passion for the job, you can usually train them in the skills on-the-job.

Now let's look at one of the three success factors and illustrate how you determine whether or not a job applicant has that quality. Specifically we will describe the process for determining whether or not a candidate has a can-do *attitude*. When a candidate has a can-do attitude, they are able to overcome obstacles; they don't blame challenges or difficulty on someone else or wait for someone else to solve the problem. They proceed to try and overcome the obstacle themselves. They may or may not be successful, but the important feature is, *they tried*.

Below is an illustration of how, during the course of an interview, we might determine whether or not an applicant has a can-do attitude.

Question to job applicant: **"Tell me about a specific time that you were struggling to get things done, but there was just not enough time. What did you do? What was the outcome?"**

As the applicant responds, listen for the following:

- **Has the applicant made any attempt to identify the priority tasks?**
- **After reviewing those items with a supervisor, were the priority tasks actually completed?**
- **Does the applicant blame the situation on a third party, like another employee or a problematic client?**
- **Does the applicant suggest that he/she needs more help to get the job done ? This is sometimes the case, but it should raise questions in your mind as an interviewer if an applicant mentions it during a job interview.**
- **Does the applicant talk about the need to get home on time ? Again, employees do have family**

obligations but it may say something more significant about an applicant who raises the issue in a job interview.

- **Does the applicant take personal responsibility for solving the problem he/she is up against or does the applicant seem to look to others to solve their problems? This suggests that an applicant has what psychologists call an "internal locus of control", a clear sign that the applicant has a high level of maturity, confidence, responsibility and problem-solving ability.**

Applicants with a can-do attitude will quickly be productive in your organization. They do not run at the first sign of trouble. They will be accountable; they don't look for other people to blame for their mistakes or their problems. They will get along with people. They will make personal adjustments in order to make things work. They finish work on time and on budget.

You can find "can-do" applicants by asking the right questions and listening carefully. In the past, you might have talked to a former employer ("a reference") but rarely is that helpful today. You can also administer pre-employment personality assessments, but it's expensive and the results may not be closely aligned with the needs of your company. So, improving your ability to interview is the choice we are left with. Few of us have ever had formal training in interviewing job applicants. But it's more important now than ever.

Carol Quinn's organization (The Hire Authority) offers an on-line course in the motivational interviewing of job applicants. It takes about four hours and costs about $300 – sometimes less. If you are serious about becoming a better interviewer of job applicants, this is a very worthwhile investment. For more information, go to Carol's website: www.hireauthority.com.

While you are looking at some specific improvements to make in your interviewing, here are several general concepts which you may find helpful:

1. Be prepared for the interview. The applicants will be prepared; you need to be prepared too. This means spending time reviewing the applicant's paperwork and preparing your own questions. Far too many times, I have initiated an interview with an applicant assuming that it was ok for me to "wing it".

2. The applicant's goal is to get a job offer or at least another interview. Your job, however, is to get as much information from the applicant as possible. Your job is not to make the applicant comfortable, except as it enables the applicant to keep talking. Your job is not to sell the organization as a great place to work; there's plenty of time for that later. Getting information should be foremost in your mind; sometimes this may mean that the discussion could take on a confrontational or adversarial tone. That's ok. Hiring is serious business and the job interview should not necessarily be a pleasant social experience.

3. Smile and nod; whether or not you agree with what the applicant has to say. The purpose of this is to encourage the applicant to keep talking. The more the applicant talks, the more information you have.

4. A talking applicant is giving you information about who they really are, but so is a quiet one. Tolerate silences. Wait out the applicant. The spacing and timing of silence might convey an important message about the strengths and weaknesses of this applicant.

5. Listen carefully. It takes a lot of energy to do this, so don't do job interviews during a time of the day when your energy level is typically down.

6. Finally, draw your specific conclusions about the person's attitude and write them down. Base your comments on the way in which they describe how they handled *specific obstacles* they have encountered in the past. Determine in advance what will constitute an answer which tells you that this is an applicant with a "can-do" attitude. When interviewing a job applicant, we want to plan the questions we are going to ask as well as the answers we want to hear.

When you hire someone, you are making a major purchase for your organization, probably at least $20,000. Think of the specifications you look for in purchasing a copier or a car or a large screen TV. Before you decide what to buy, you try to have a pretty clear picture of how the product will perform. Make sure you know whether or not this applicant can do the job, and delay the decision until you are comfortable about it, one way or another.

Finally, organizations should look at personnel decisions with an eye toward quality improvement. Hiring managers should coach each other on interviewing skills and should meet to review the quality of their hire decisions. A measure might be whether or not the number of 6 month terminations is decreasing. Your ability to meet a goal like this will have a lot to do with your ability to provide a success experience for clients. In addition, staff tenure strongly correlates with staff satisfaction… staff happiness. More experienced staff are easier to work with because they have the ability and experience to carry their share of the workload. Productivity is higher. Everybody wins.

For Discussion

1. Think about your last job interview. How would you evaluate the interviewer? How much did he/she know about you when you left? Were your most important qualities/deficits for the job discussed?
2. How does your organization do on hiring effectiveness? What percentage of your hires are still employed and doing well after the first year of employment? What would you like that percentage to be?
3. When you are interviewing someone, does silence bother you? Have you ever left an applicant "off the hook"? Do you want the applicant to feel comfortable with you?
4. What is your organization doing to ensure that hiring decisions are made consistently from one hiring manager to the next?
5. Do you have a standardized format for interviewing applicants; i.e. a structured list of questions to ask as well as issues not to discuss?
6. What is your opinion: how important is a "can-do" attitude to job success?
7. Has your organization ever considered pre-hire personality testing as a screening tool? Why or why not have you implemented that idea?

NOTES

two

Appoint Great Supervisors and Support Them

"Supervision is an opportunity to bring someone back to their own mind, to show them how good they can be."
-Nancy Kline

Human service supervisors are in a tough spot. Rarely were they selected for their leadership ability and yet they are roundly criticized when they fail to be true leaders. Recent studies suggest that 53% of senior executives are unhappy with the work being done by front line supervisors.

Those who become supervisors are often the people who stuck with the job, worked the extra hours and didn't tire. They came to work on time, got the job done without abusing anyone and were usually able to get along with people. Then one day they came to work and learned that they had been promoted to being a supervisor. Wow! Suddenly they are supervising former colleagues who in some cases were friends, or neighbors or even relatives. It is a tough transition and one that often they are left to struggle with alone.

Many supervisors tell me that they talk to their direct reports "all the time." When you push a little harder you find out that this means they say hello passing in the hallway or make casual comments to each other on other informal occasions. This is not supervision.

Supervision involves teaching someone how to improve their performance and it does not happen informally. It cannot happen until two or more people meet each other in a safe, confidential setting where individual performance issues can be discussed. It's a process that benefits everyone, regardless of their skill level. Sometimes "group supervision" works well but normally it's a 1:1 situation.

What roles do supervisors play in your organization? If I were about to become a member of your staff and you were going to assign me to your "best supervisor" – who would that be and why? And, why would I want to work for that person? What do they bring to the table in terms of supervision; in terms of skills, abilities and attributes that I might be able to learn from? After a month working for your "best supervisor", would I be likely to view my decision to join your organization as a good one or will I dread the day that I darkened your door? Over time, employees develop intense feelings about their supervisor. They may be very annoyed, frustrated or humiliated by that person. Or, hopefully, they are grateful and loyal because their supervisor has been key to their success.

According to a variety of studies, a large percentage – at least half – of employees do not trust their supervisor. They believe supervisors lie to save their own reputation; violate confidentiality; are rarely accountable; and lack follow through on their commitments. 75% of terminating workers blame a poor relationship with their supervisor as the main reason they are going to work for another organization. Supervisors need the ability to work with people.

There are supervisors who are successful. They are good listeners; they are willing to let ideas flow from others and they are accountable. They are good communicators even under pressure. They do not loose emotional control or say whatever comes to mind. Their communication, the words they choose and how they are stated, is purposeful, designed to accomplish something positive for the organization and its clients. The following seven behaviors illustrate in a more concrete fashion the general qualities I have just described.

1. They are good communicators, even under pressure. They do not lose emotional control or say whatever comes to mind. Their communication, the words they choose and how they are stated, is purposeful, designed to accomplish something positive.

2. They do not play 'favorites'. They may be seen as "tough" or "easy" but if they are fair and consistent, they will earn the respect of their direct reports.

3. They are good at delegation. They look for new ways to get the work done. They tap into the strengths of their direct reports. They teach and make sure the person will be successful at completing the new assignment.

4. They don't throw staff "under the bus". They take personal responsibility when things go wrong and don't look for a direct report to blame. Later, what went wrong can be discussed.

5. They make others look good. Their direct reports often are recipients of awards and greater compensation. They are teachers and mentors and not enforcers. They find tremendous satisfaction when their direct reports do well. One of the biggest thrills of my career was when one of my direct reports was able to double his salary in two years.

6. They are learners. They lead by example. They don't just instruct their employees to go to workshops and seminars;

they go themselves. They are committed to quality and their own development. They demonstrate their personal commitment to be a better supervisor today than they were yesterday.

7. Learners yes, but teachers too. That is they see their role as helping direct reports learn how to successfully complete their work. They are not just a "cop" wanting to catch someone making a mistake.

Many supervisors today are learning to be "teachers." Through experience they have quickly learned that the old fashioned "command and control" structure is no longer effective in the long haul. Today's employees have different workplace expectations. They expect the workplace to be a pleasant, even a fun experience and are not prepared to be hollered at or ordered to do this job or that. They want their work experience to be aligned with the rest of their lives which are often organized around a sense of fulfillment, psychological balance, personal growth and a positive blend of work and personal life. They want to be involved in solving problems; to have their ideas heard. Things will not go well, if supervisors are simply telling them what to do without considering their input.

But if supervisors can't holler at people to get work done properly, or it doesn't work to do it that way, how do they motivate and get the respect and cooperation that is required. One way is that they make a commitment to the success of their employees and are very open about it. When an employee gets a promotion they view it as a sign of supervisory success; when an employee is having a performance issue or leaves during the first year, the supervisor doesn't stand around and criticize that employee but they look at what really is going wrong and how it might have been handled differently. What did the employee need from the supervisor, if anything, that they did not receive?

Good supervisors have low tolerances for poor performance. In this sense they can look like "enforcers" but it's all about intent. They call attention to performance issues quickly so that the employee can learn quickly without further issues which might damage the work experience and career. In other words, they are proactive, stopping small problems before they become larger. The typical situation in most organizations is that when an employee's performance begins to slide, it continues till it reaches the point of significant discipline or even termination. It's a process we need to improve...changing employee performance for the better. We are able to do that with many clients; now it is time that we excel at changing employee behavior too.

Talking with an employee about their negative performance was always difficult for me. Most of us struggle at some level with confrontation and conflict. It's probably something we bring to the job from our own birth families. In my career, I found many reasons to delay confronting an employee about their less-than-satisfactory performance. My excuses all seemed legitimate; the employee was still new, or I knew they had a rough day, or it was Friday and I didn't want to ruin their weekend, or I knew they were having a hard time off the job. In truth, my delay rationale was not fair to the employee, the organization or myself. It is like a cut finger; if it is cleaned and treated quickly, infection can normally be avoided.

Finally, supervisors need support. They need help with the adjustment to being the boss in the first place. When initially appointed, supervisors don't know what their duties really are, despite what it may say in the job description. They do not feel comfortable in the role and don't know how to handle it. Consequently without a mentor to coach them along the way, they little by little morph back into being an entry level employee, where they do feel comfortable and know what is expected. All of a sudden a senior level manager realizes that there is an entire area of the operation which is essentially unsupervised, and you have a supervisor who is earning more money but not being a supervisor.

How can supervisors be helped and supported? How can they grow professionally and personally so that they really are the leaders of your organization? This will require an investment of time and/or money which will however, pay off in terms of the performance of the organization on the front lines. Perhaps an experienced supervisor, who is willing to give a "rookie" some special attention, can play an invaluable role in the success of a new supervisor. Or the services of a leadership coach who understands the needs of the supervisor (or a group of supervisors) can be an invaluable factor in organizational improvement. In social services we are beginning to see the retention of coaches for senior managers. The organization needs to recognize that when things go wrong on the front lines and there is an insufficient attention to detail at that level, the consequences for the organization can be enormous. Perhaps the most helpful feature will be the attitude of the senior leadership of the organization who understand that because an employee was a good front line, direct service worker, does not automatically mean that they will be a successful front line supervisor.

For Discussion

1. As you think back on your career and reflect upon supervisors that you have had in the past, what were the characteristics that made them a good supervisor? Why do you regard some of them in less than favorable terms? What happened to you professionally during those times when you admired your supervisor? What new skills did you learn? What new experiences did you have? On the other hand, what happened to you under the tutelage of someone you did not respect? What was your attitude like? How was your morale? How was your productivity?

2. How would you evaluate supervisors?

3. Do you feel that supervisors should be held accountable for the performance of their direct reports?

4. What does your organization do to help supervisors improve? How do you help them cope with the stress of a job where people about you and below you are very eager to be critical, or so it seems some days?

5. In your organization, what are the symptoms of supervisory success or what are the symptoms of supervisor inadequacy?

6. Are people promoted into supervisory positions because they possess the competency to be a supervisor or is the promotion the organization's way of saying thank you for an entry level job well done?

NOTES

three

Help New Employees Feel Welcome

" The beginning is the most important part of the work."
-Plato

"On-boarding...helps the new employee to feel socially comfortable...to feel like they belong."
-L. Wenger

In the corporate human resources world, there's a new buzz word – "on-boarding." Oversimplified this refers to what happens in the employee's first few months on the job, that makes him/her feel welcome. The non-profit world has not really given this too much attention; yet, at least. But when we take the time to look, it's obvious that on-boarding programs could make a big difference for non-profits, just like they have been doing in the traditional corporate world for years now. Good on-boarding programs allow new employees to learn the new job expectations more quickly. They encourage engagement or a sense of excitement about the new job and they reduce costs through lower turnover rates and the related expense; fewer new employees are leaving unexpectedly during the first few months. A lack of on-boarding results in the scenario where a new employee on his/her first day, goes to lunch and never returns and no one knows why. Probably many of you have seen this happen.

On-boarding is not the same as orientation. Orientation is very important. It provides the new employee with information about the organization, its mission, values, policies, procedures and expectations.

On-boarding procedures however, help the new employee to feel socially comfortable...to feel like they belong. Children who go to school for the first time, especially if it is a new school, feel out of place, like everyone is watching them; they feel alone and isolated, not part of the group. New employees can feel the same way and when they do, there is a proportionate delay in how long it will take them to become a truly productive member of the workforce.

I have changed jobs many times in my career. One of the best orientations I ever received was in the early 1980's. My new employer used an entire week to help us understand the scope of work being addressed by the organization. I was very impressed by all the important people who came in to talk with the new group of employees. I learned a lot during that week. So the organization's goal had been largely accomplished. But I also forgot a lot of what was said...my mind simply could not retain all of the information that was thrown at us in a short period of time.

Despite all of this emphasis on orientation, I still felt very new and still had lots of questions and concerns. It wasn't that I needed more factual information, what I needed was a feeling of confidence and re-assurance. Where could I go to lunch? Who would go to lunch with me? Is the neighborhood dangerous? Did people around here leave at 5 or were you expected to work late? Several hundred people worked in the building; how would I ever get to know them all? Would they like me? Would they be able to pronounce my name? Will they trust me? Will they think the scar on my neck is ugly? Will I get a chance to show them what I can do? How will it be when I make a mistake?

In fairness to my new employer, there was a part of me that was on "cloud 9." Why? Well, about two weeks before I started I got a phone call from my boss. She told me that they were going to re-paint the space that was to be my office and did I have any color preferences. That is the only time something like that has ever happened before or since and I was truly impressed.

It seems pretty typical however for new employees in to go through a 6 month adjustment period. Sometimes this adjustment is pretty smooth. Often the new employee is excited about the new job and for a few months will even overlook issues that might otherwise be of concern; it can be a "honeymoon" period.

Colleagues are sometimes warm and welcoming, but I have heard too many stories that suggest that the welcome was anything but warm. Newcomers have little or no contact with their supervisor; sometimes colleagues actually say things like, "you don't have what it takes to work here." New employees are sometimes expected to prove themselves before others will let them "in" to the group. It's a sink or swim proposition. So in a situation like this, when the new employee goes home at the end of the day, how should he/she respond to their family's question, "how was your first day at work?"

The first six months is critical. If you examine turnover events you will see that if an employee can survive the first six months, there is a good chance they will be there for several years. And in the non-profit world where entry level turnover can be more than 50%, an employee who lasts 2-3 years can be a real asset. The 2013 Gallup survey on employee engagement tells us that only 30% of employees are truly excited about their work. In the best of worlds, the employee's enthusiasm about the job is higher during the first six months. The survey indicates that at the six month point, employee engagement and motivation is typically about 50% or 20 points better than employees as a whole. So it is after six months when engagement levels begin to fall, slowly but surely to the 30% level. However, on-boarding programs help to continue the engagement momentum because they provide the new employee with:

- Exposure to senior managers who are (hopefully) engaged at a high level
- The opportunity to see how other employees are encouraged to grow and learn new skills
- Encouragement to develop meaningful social relationships amongst co-workers
- Seeing first hand how the organization can benefit its employees

Recently, HR Blogger Ron Thomas identified standardized on-boarding procedures that organizations can use to help new employees feel welcome. These should be incorporated into a clear policy and procedure statement which articulates how the organization will help in the adjustment of a new employee. Helping new employees adjust is the *organization's* job and should not be contingent on the personality of the particular supervisor to whom the employee is assigned.

Here are some of Ron's suggestions:

1. Even before the employee starts, have a colleague-to-be send a welcome note or email.
2. If the employee is assigned desk and office space, make sure it is clean and ready including an initial stock of supplies.
3. Be there to welcome them on the first day (the most important of the employee's tenure) and introduce them to other key people they will interact with.
4. Debrief with them at the end of each day for at least the first two weeks.

5. Give them something from the organization to take home and share with the family; perhaps just a formal invitation to visit and get a guided tour of the organization.
6. Begin the process of setting long term goals and objectives.
7. Review the job description.
8. Conclude the first week with a lunch or coffee and donuts for the new employee and the assigned work group.
9. Have realistic expectations. In the first several weeks, perhaps the first several months, they may be able to actually contribute very little. A new job is one of life's major stressors and "first day jitters" may last quite a while. But nonetheless, make them feel welcome as a person so that later they are more inclined to really dig in.
10. Make initial assignments a combination of small and easy-to-accomplish to large and more complex; be ready to support their performance on the complex work and praise their accomplishment with the smaller tasks.
11. At least every 30 days make it a point to meet with the employee and assess their level of comfort with the organization. This assessment should include the extent of social comfort as well as comfort with the characteristics of the tasks assigned.

While many of the welcoming duties fall to the new employee's supervisor, the supervisor should not be left on his/her own in terms of how the welcoming experience is designed. Some supervisors will simply be stronger than others in terms of meeting the social needs of new employees. Organizations must have a standardized way to help new employees feel welcome. Finally, recognize that the new on-boarding program will not be perfect on the initial roll-out. Most new programs require modification before they are "right." If 6 months turnover continues to be higher than you want, even with a new on-boarding program in place, collect supervisors in one room, get their feedback about how the on-boarding program is working and make modifications. Their experience in implementing the on-boarding program will be invaluable when it comes to improving it. A six-month status review is a good idea for an on-boarding program, or any program for that matter, whether or not the program is new. Make changes, freshen it up; demonstrate your commitment to ongoing quality improvement.

For Discussion

1. Talk about some of your experiences as a new employee with your current job or a job you previously held. Remember those uncomfortable first few days?

2. What did your employer do that helped you to feel more comfortable? Or did you continue to feel alone and isolated for awhile?

3. As you survey your present organization how do you think new employees are being treated? Sometimes new employees are not treated well because they are seen as taking extra work or overtime away from the current group. Have you ever seen that happen?

4. What might keep your organization from implementing an on-boarding program?

5. If you were going to start an on-boarding program, what features would it contain?

6. How do you think technology could be used to help new employees feel more welcome?

NOTES

four

Delegate Tasks Successfully

**"Surround yourself with the best people you can find,
delegate authority, and don't interfere as long as the
policy you've decided upon is being carried out."**
-Ronald Reagan

In the mid-80's I worked for a social service organization that provided services on an international level. I traveled frequently to new and developing program sites in Canada, Central America and throughout the U.S. After I had worked there about three weeks, the CEO called me to his office the night before I was to take my first trip to Toronto. He handed me an envelope and said, "Deliver this $15,000 check to John at the main office." What a hoot. $15,000 was and is a lot of money and here I was, the "green horn" on the staff, being asked by the CEO to deliver this check to an important person in Toronto. I walked out of the office, envelope in hand, as though I was walking on air. It had been a long time since anyone had handed me such a compliment.

So it goes with delegation. It is an opportunity to acknowledge staff who work for you, and from whom you expect bigger things from in the future. When you delegate a task to someone, you express your confidence in them and in effect provide recognition for the excellent work they have done in the past.

What is delegation? Jana S. Ferris of the Washington State University Extension says that *"delegation is getting others to do your work, so you can get to what you are really supposed to be doing."* Non-profits are well known for having everyone help when there is a job that needs to be done and staffing is short. Sometimes staff members don't really know what they are supposed to be doing; they are so used to wearing many different hats that they are no longer sure which hat is theirs. They have lost all sight of their priorities.

But, things are changing. Increasingly non-profits are paying more attention to who is supposed to do what and they are trying to help staff develop skills around a particular set of tasks – in other words, the workforce is becoming more specialized. The change I believe is driven by an increasing attention to outcomes. Funding is following satisfactory outcomes in this day and age and staff have become more focused in their approach to day to day tasks.

So in this age of specialization, successful delegation is something that many non-profit staff may have to learn about. In the increasingly competitive marketplace in which non-profits operate, learning to delegate will have advantages. It's not the "do whatever" approach to delegation that might have been true in the past; delegation can and should be a special skill that managers and supervisors use to advance the goals of the organization. Successful delegation leads to:

- higher staff retention;
- burnout prevention;
- staff who develop new skills;
- the emergence of a systems approach;

- the use of teams to get things done rather than assignments taken on solely by individuals.
- the identification of skills which to this point have gone unnoticed.

Sometimes there is resistance to delegation. Why? What are the reasons why we do not delegate? Here are some of more commonly heard reasons for not delegating:

- It's too hard.
- It takes too much time; "easier to do it myself."
- Nobody can do it as good as I can.
- Nobody else has any time either.
- If I delegate too much, will I be needed?

No doubt these statements sound familiar. They are understandable reasons in many cases. However, I think they are most often heard from people who don't realize the technology of delegation or rather the technology of *successful delegation*.

So how does one successfully delegate? There are six steps in successful delegation; you can easily remember them with the acronym, IDEALS.

1. **Introduce the task** and clearly identify the assigned responsibility. Especially if it is a difficult task, a manager may run the risk of making the assignment sound easier than it is in order to ensure that there is less resistance from the staff member. Be honest and clear regarding the assignment that you are asking someone to help with.
2. **Demonstrate what needs to be done**. Provide clear verbal and written directions; role play it; do a "dry run". As much as possible, prepare the staff member for the experience of doing the job successfully. To give an assignment to someone not prepared is to pave the way for their failure.

3. **Ensure understanding**. Ask the staff member to review the job he/she has been assigned and the various steps that might be involved. This feedback will tell you whether or not you have done a good job of demonstrating and explaining.

4. **Allocate resources**: authority, information, money. Give the staff member the tools they need to do a good job. If the employee is to assume supervisory responsibility, make sure other staff know that he/she has been given the authority to act as such. Make sure the staff member knows the limits of authority; what can or cannot be decided without outside consultation.

5. **Let go**. Now that you have given the task, have given instructions, and provided the necessary resources let the staff member do the job assigned without unnecessary interference. The staff member may not do the job in exactly the same manner that you would have done it. That's ok as long as the desired outcome is met. In fact, it is possible that another way of doing something could lead to greater effectiveness and efficiency.

6. **Support and Monitor.** Finally, hold the staff member accountable. This underlines the importance of what they have done. You see, delegation is about more than getting work done, although that is important. Delegation is about telling a staff that their skills are acknowledged; that they have earned your trust. If you do not follow-up however, the message to the staff member is that the job you gave them to do was not very important. Sometimes it seems, we are just too busy to provide this kind of support and other times we just assume that if we don't hear anything, everything must have gone ok. It's the "let sleeping dogs lie" approach and it's very dangerous. Often it did not go well and that is the reason we have not heard anything. When you delegate, make this kind of follow-up a priority. In the long run, it will save you time.

By using the above guidelines you will be able to begin to delegate successfully. Start delegating right away. Don't wait till you are feeling overwhelmed and on the verge of burnout to start thinking about delegating some responsibilities; almost certainly it will not go well. Do some delegation when you are not feeling overwhelmed, when you are thinking clearly and can take the time to do a thorough job of it. Look for people who are ready for more responsibility. It's a compliment to them. And there are benefits to you too: it will keep you from being a turnover statistic, and will get you home in time for dinner.

For Discussion

1. When was the last time you delegated a task, and what was the outcome?

2. Are there tasks you should not delegate? Think about and discuss some examples.

3. Has anyone ever refused to accept a delegated task? Did they have a good reason?

4. Do you find it hard to allow someone to satisfactorily complete a task, because they did not do it in the same way you might have done it?

5. When you delegate a task, do you think it's a good idea to let everyone on your team know that you are delegating a task you normally do, to one particular team member? Why?

6. What factors keep you from delegating more frequently?

NOTES

five

Happy Hour is 9-5. Have Fun

**"I love deadlines. I love the whooshing
noise they make as they go by."
- Douglas Adams**

The title of this chapter does not originate with me. I borrowed it from Alexander Kjerulf, who is a self proclaimed *Chief Happiness Officer*. He wrote a book, <u>Happy Hour is 9-5.</u> It's a great title because it pushes us to think about the workplace in a whole different light. Even if you are not a "happy hour person", you get the point. Your employees can, and should, truly enjoy being at work. Your employees spend more time with each other than anyone else during their waking hours. It would be too bad if they dreaded their time together.

Some social service workers truly enjoy their work. However, I continue to hear about people who dread coming to work for a number of reasons: supervisors and managers who take advantage of their employees; people being disrespected; extremely heavy workloads; lack of formal supervision; too much paperwork and unmotivated coworkers who are just putting in time.

What I rarely hear about is employees who work in a place where the employer goes out of his/her way to make work fun.

In my introduction to this book, I mentioned the Pike Place Fish Market in Seattle, where minimum wage workers, in a cold and wet fish market manage to have fun on the job.

Let me be clear, about fun. It is not when people stand around the coffee pot or water cooler and are caught up in laughter; often this is laughter which is at the expense of other staff or clients; that's staff making fun of each other and it's not funny. My definition of having fun on the job is when enjoyable things happen during the work day that completely takes your mind off of current duties. It's a break to get rejuvenated. They are about rejuvenation of the workforce; the activity, timing and setting are not random or accidental; it is planned. Planned, but not contrived or manipulated; not forced fun. The organization must devote resources to a process like this or it does not happen... or it happens accidentally and without consistency. That's why Tony Hsieh, CEO of Zappos talks about their corporate value of "fun and a little weirdness." Creating fun in the workplace is a management responsibility and in the case of Zappos, "fun" is the beginning of superior customer service.

What is more typical however is that management allows discouragement to continue. Management allows depressing things to occur and to continue. In some cases they create them. I know managers who, for years, have been complaining about lazy, unmotivated workers; about high turnover, and about the demanding new generation of employees. Yet, it's rare that managers get together to figure out a strategy to change these situations. They just see these employee performance issues as part of the cost of doing business. They complain about the fact that they can't afford to pay people more - as if a raise would actually put smiles on people's faces for very long. Human service agencies should be leading the way on employee morale issues and too often they are not. But what a difference it could make if leaders could turn their thinking in a completely different direction by designing their workplaces to be centers of smiles, harmony, cooperation, and by creating a true spirit of family. The real problem is that many times, management does not see fun as a legitimate part of their business strategy. They see employees as already getting away with too much...too much down time. They are not even sure that "fun" should be part of work. Their beliefs may have "protestant work ethic roots"...life ought to be about hard work, striving and sacrifice, not fun. This is an idea that has outlived its usefulness; fun needs to be a part of the social service workplace.

So what should we be doing to make it a real blast to come to work? What would your workplace look like if it was designed for fun? What will move an organization's culture in that direction?

1. Start by reading Alexander Kierulf's book.
2. Look at YouTube videos on the Pike Place Fish Market in Seattle. There you have low wage workers having fun on the job. What would your workplace look like if fun was a part of your culture? I challenge you to work on that. It will take determination; early measures may not demonstrate success. No one formula will work in every work culture. But keep trying! You will find the formula that is right for your organization.
3. Forget about this time-honored tradition of keeping business and personal relationships separate; supervisors and employees will get to know each other personally and they will celebrate each other's accomplishments and support each other during difficult times. They will be familiar with each other's non-work interests. This is not nosiness or a lack of respecting employee-supervisory boundaries. This is simply recognizing that people, on the job or off, can be of help to each other.
4. Supervisors would be trained in their primary responsibility...that of developing positive relationships with their

direct reports and investing in their skill development. They would be seen laughing and crying together; celebrating success, and supporting each other during failures and mistakes. This is the foundation for problem solving, "how could we do it better next time". Supervisors would spend more effort acknowledging the good work that people do and less effort on finding their mistakes.

5. Supervisors should be asking themselves, "What kind of workplace have I created that my staff would want to work here"? Or, what kind of supervisor am I that someone would want to work for me? Supervisors should be committed to being a better leader tomorrow than they were today.

6. There would be an atmosphere of "listening". As much as we focus on saying the right words, we should even more develop the skills of listening. Our listening should be in both formal and informal settings. Listening will help reshape the workplace so that it is truly a friendly place for everyone.

7. There would be a lot of job sharing and cross training. People should be encouraged to help each other succeed. Managers would help out when coverage is too tight. As much as possible, everyone would understand the demands of other jobs, not just their own.

8. Look for smiling faces; listen for laughter; reward honesty (even when it hurts). Make **fun** an organization value. Your organization will become **the place to work in your community.**

I know that as a human service leader, you are always concerned with tight budgets. Surprisingly, you will find that many of these things do not cost a lot. Yet, there are a multitude of payoffs for creating a fun work culture – primarily a happy, productive, cooperative, confident, proud and successful team of staff members who will enjoy working for you.

Here is a list of fun things that can take place in the workplace that are not expensive.

- Costume day
- Pizza afternoon; invite families – sometimes you may need to take employees away from their families; here's an opportunity to include them
- A 5-minute monologue from a late night comedian that suddenly appears on the organization's computer network.
- Nerf gun wars (finance vs. case managers)
- Snooze stations
- Desk chair massages
- Changing desk assignments for the day
- 15 minute karaoke break
- Everyone gets to show their favorite silly YouTube video
- Appoint a humor officer of the week
- Start a video game tournament

Solicit other ideas (including off-the-wall ideas) from your employees. If you don't ask, you'll just be guessing about what might be rejuvenating for them.

For Discussion

1. When was the last time your workgroup really had fun together? What did you do that made it an especially enjoyable time? Was it worth the cost?
2. Do you think that professional boundaries are crossed when your group is having fun? Why or why not?
3. Do you feel comfortable sharing personal information with co-workers?
4. Do you think that more "fun" would make your organization more productive? How can it happen without costing a lot of money?
5. Can smiling be encouraged and reinforced?
6. What happens or what might happen when people engage in 5 minutes of silliness at your office?

NOTES

six

Stop the Blame Game

It's time to care; it's time to take responsibility; it's time to lead; it's time for a change; it's time to be true to our greatest self; it's time to stop blaming others."
- Steve Maraboli

Blame has been hanging around since the beginning of time. Adam tried to blame Eve when he ate the forbidden fruit; then Eve promptly pointed to the serpent. The "Blame Game" describes a phenomenon that pervades today's culture. We are always looking for someone or something to blame for the mess in which we find ourselves.

Recently a young man being served by an organization for persons with disabilities died after he was left in an overheated van following a trip to the movies. In the investigation which followed, everyone pointed the finger at everyone else. In the final analysis, one staff member actually went to jail. Who knows where the fault really lies, and how this tragedy actually happened, but newspaper accounts clearly illustrated a common pattern of responsibility avoidance, where everyone pointed the finger at everyone else for this terrible tragedy.

By definition, blame is to hold another person or group responsible for perceived faults, real, imagined or invented. It is an act of censure, reproach and often outright condemnation.

Blame is used to place responsibility and accountability for faults on another person or group. And in its extreme form, blame is a form of scapegoating…"it's YOU that caused all this mess to happen."

The motivation behind blaming is certainly understandable. People don't like to confront their own mistakes or lose face. They don't want to jeopardize their job, career or reputation. In hierarchical organizations, blame can be a very effective way of pushing a mistake off on to someone else. It is very common however, in organizations where the stress level is high; where there is little vertical communication and where there is an absence of trust.

The Blame Game is usually fed by management. Within the culture of an organization, the blame game can become the way that mistakes are handled. In a blaming environment, someone (individuals/group) has to take the heat instead of looking at the policies, procedures, systems, lack of training and inadequate staff development as incubators of accidents waiting to happen…mistakes waiting to be made. The worst part about shifting the blame, pointing the finger or finding a "fall guy" is that it distracts everyone from finding out what really caused the problem and how to stop it from reoccurring. Blaming stops organizations from looking at how to prevent problems.

Another real life example of how this works in an organization is from the following story. Every other Friday afternoon there was a scramble to get time sheets submitted in time for payroll to be prepared and delivered the following week. Collecting time sheets at this organization was especially complex since program sites were spread over several counties. HR staff, who normally pulled time sheets together for the payroll report, openly blamed Program Directors in outlying counties for not sending their time sheets on time. Those same Program Directors always insisted that the time sheets had been faxed to central office in a timely manner. When all the finger pointing stopped, it was discovered that time sheets were being sent to three different fax machines and ended up laying around on people's desks for hours before being sent to HR. Specifying the one fax machine to use and having a clear protocol for delivering faxed time sheets to HR fixed the problem. But it was not getting solved as long as everyone was pointing the finger at other people.

Gerald Weinberg, systems theorist, holds that the flow of blame in an organization is an important indicator of the organization's robustness and integrity. Weinberg believes that if blame is allowed to flow upward, it proves that management takes responsibility and is willing to supply staff with the resources required to do their job. Further, he argues that blame flowing downward from management to staff or laterally between colleagues is a sign of organizational failure.

Social services must learn to go beyond the blame game by examining procedures in place in other high risk settings such as in military ground operations, on aircraft carriers, in guided missile or drone operations, nuclear power plants and more recently hospitals and general health care settings. In these settings we have learned the importance of going beyond blame; it's safe to admit mistakes, report failures and near misses. Small mistakes are not ignored...because if not corrected they lead to larger mistakes with more calamitous outcomes. Appreciate the value of near misses; they should be treated as organizational blessings because they represent an opportunity to learn and improve.

Social workers need to learn to anticipate possible failure; staff need to look at what could go wrong in a service delivery process and to continually be thinking of new avenues of care and service which are safer and more effective.

Social service agencies who want to stop the blame game will have the following characteristics:

- Communication must be improved. Sometimes there is a lack of understanding about why a particular strategy was employed.
- It must be safe to discuss problems; staff meetings should begin with a review of what went wrong and how it could be fixed.
- Organizations must work at telling the truth from top to bottom; no staff member is exempt from this requirement; to do this there must be a high trust level – trust that telling the truth will not be subject to reprimand or punishment. A recent article in Inc. magazine, described a U.K. company where on a monthly basis, employees voluntarily come to a makeshift company "chapel" to confess their sins; to acknowledge the on-the-job mistakes they have made during the last month and to describe what they are going to do to correct that in the future. After each "confession" the other assembled employees burst into loud applause, celebrating the courage and determination of the confessing employee. It's an interesting way to not only make truth-telling acceptable but highly desirable; behavior to be reinforced.
- Someone on staff should become an expert at Root Cause Analysis and other problem-solving, decision making procedures.
- There must be a cultural atmosphere of transparency. This increases the possibility that everyone knows what is going on and opens up additional avenues for suggestions and corrective, problem-avoiding feedback. When managers make all the decisions without input from those affected, the stage is set for unforeseen problems to develop.

- The expectation should be that if there is an opportunity for a mistake, sooner or later it will happen. Too many organizations take the opposite form…"everything will be ok, if nobody screws up".
- Finally, the most important point of all, recognize that mistakes are sometimes the result of system failures and not merely personal inadequacies on the part of employees. Just like the consumer conscious manufacturer who builds a product to be used as most consumers will use them. But their product will not always be used by consumers who exercise good judgment or care. Their product must withstand abuse because that is how it is sometimes going to be used. In a similar vein organizational systems must be designed to be as fail-safe as possible.

Managers must work to discourage blame. Creating a culture where blame is not the first recourse is hard work. But a blame-free culture is a rich environment in which staff will be able to work together in new and exciting ways.

For Discussion

1. When was the last time you were blamed for something that went wrong? How did blame contribute to or detract from your sense of well-being?
2. In your organization, can people who are responsible for mistakes be counted on to accept accountability?
3. Does your organization have a formal model for reviewing incidents to determine what went wrong and to avoid future errors? If so, how would you evaluate its effectiveness? If not, do you believe it would be helpful to adopt a model for incident review?
4. Can you think of a time when it was easier to blame an individual employee than get to the root of the problem?
5. As a manager, what has been your experience with blame? Is it the response of choice when something goes wrong or is it replaced with problem analysis and learning?
6. What steps might your organization take to shift from blame to learning?

NOTES

seven

Learn to Trust Each Other

"Trust is the lubrication that makes it possible for organizations to work."
- Warren Bennis

Learning to trust our co-workers may be the next frontier in human service staff development. In today's society, we have a crisis of trust. A 2010 study revealed that 9 of 10 employees had experienced a breach of trust on the job. Everyone is skeptical and suspicious. Employees don't trust their supervisors. Nobody trusts politicians and only about half of us trust the military, the clergy or police. Trusting others is a major challenge but if we can develop and maintain trusting relationships, both on and off the job, we will be more successful. Trust enables honesty and facilitates problem-solving.

What is the level of trust in your organization? Here are some questions that can help you assess whether or not your employees trust each other.

- How comfortable are people with each other?
- Are your employees able to admit their mistakes and give each other honest feedback?

- Do staff members speak their honest opinion when a controversial subject is under discussion?
- Is everyone guarded in their conversation and careful about the words they use?
- Do people share their personal struggles or do we pretend that our personal problems don't make a difference at work?

Trust makes all the difference in an organization. Warren Buffet once said, "Trust is like the air we breathe. When it's present, no one really notices, but when it is absent, everybody notices." Three characteristics seem to be present in high trust organizations:

- Employees see everyone (especially management) as credible.
- Employees experience respect.
- Employees believe they are treated fairly.

All of this leads to better financial performance for high-trust organizations. In tracking 100 high-trust, publicly traded companies, they were found to outperform the S&P 500.

Team-building guru Patrick Lencioni says that trusting relationships form the basis of work teams being able to work together successfully. Further, he recommends that work teams intentionally develop the ability to trust one another because when they do, their work is geometrically more successful. Yet, learning to develop and maintain trust is difficult because we are all human and make mistakes. Developing trust in co-workers on a team is no different than the process of learning to trust others in the context of our personal relationships. We learn to trust people who do what they say they will do; who follow up; who are honest and whose behavior is consistent. We learn to trust people who support us; who are fair with us; who pick us up when we fall. People we trust don't vary their description of an event based on who they are talking to. These are the qualities that build trust, on and off the job. Trust breaks down when the opposite of these qualities are exhibited. Restoring broken trust, as we know from our personal lives, is difficult, but it can be done. Restoring broken trust simply requires that all of the qualities that build trust in the first place be exhibited only with more intensity...and probably over a long period of time. When leaders, or anyone, violate trust, the first thing they need to do is to acknowledge this mistake; until that happens, the trust rebuilding process cannot begin.

Four organizational values set the stage for the development of trusting relationships amongst staff:

1. employees do what they say they are going to do;
2. trust and truthfulness are organizational core values and are re-enforced by day to day decision-making;
3. there is a commitment on the part of all employees, top to bottom, to learn from mistakes, to perform better today than yesterday;
4. fear and blame are eliminated

Once those characteristics are in place, staff are able to carry out some very simple activities that develop trust. For example, in team meetings, team members should be encouraged to share their personal stories including memorable events in their past as well as challenging situations which developed more recently. Also, team members can take a personality assessment which identifies the strengths and weaknesses of their respective temperaments.

I recommend the Keirsey Temperament Sorter; it's simple and inexpensive and gives everyone a description of their own temperament style along with the strengths and weaknesses of that style. For example, some are especially creative and are good at developing new solutions to old problems. Others are good at maintaining a system that someone else has developed. Knowing individual temperament strengths enables better task assignment and more likely task completion. Being aware of our differences, our strengths and weaknesses, helps to make logical job assignments. When we not only accept but leverage our differences we greatly increase the possibility that we can accomplish the mission of the organization.

Whenever employees get to know each other better, a stronger bond develops amongst the group and trust increases. They become more able to discuss program-related issues honestly, openly and productively. This happens because they have deliberately practiced honesty with each other. It does not develop by pushing a button; it takes intentional practice and like any trusting relationship, from time to time it requires maintenance.

I always encourage work teams to directly discuss their failures. When staff meetings happen, it is far too easy for us to act like there are no problems; when the truth is, we all know there are problems, sometimes many. Discussing failures enables learning to occur. Someone once told me, when you go skiing, the only way to become better is to fall down from time to time; "if you're not falling, you're not learning." So rather than beginning our meetings with, "how are things going?" why not start with "what has gone wrong this week... where are we struggling?" Not only do we learn from looking at our failures, but when we are comfortable discussing our failures with team members, it allows for feelings of trust to be nourished.

Higher levels of trust will make a big difference in your organization. Here is what you can expect after you have spent some time being very intentional about developing trust:

- Staff will demonstrate increased skill at whatever their job requires.
- We will learn how to do things better the next time.
- Employee satisfaction will be higher and turnover lower.
- The services we provide will reach a higher level of quality.
- Staff meetings will be exciting and incredibly productive.
- Everyone will feel free to express themselves and the truly best idea will emerge.

Finally, we can benefit from the creativity of Corsum Consulting who in 2009 developed these 5 methods that leaders can use to develop trust throughout the organization.

T = Teach. Teach everyone in the organization how things work; make it as transparent as possible.

R = Reward. Make sure reward systems align with corporate values and goals.

U = Unconditional support. Encourage innovation. Create an environment where mistakes are opportunities to learn, not to punish. Give employees permission to "think outside the box". Adopt a value of love and concern and allow it to replace criticism and condemnation.

S = Share information. Communicate clearly and frequently. No secrets.

T = Trustworthy. Make commitments and keep them.

Let's get serious about learning to trust each other. It may seem like a pretty "soft" skill but research done by the Flagler Business School at the University of North Carolina tells us that "high trust" corporations are also the ones doing the best financially. As non-profit providers we may not be so concerned with out profit margins, although we should certainly be concerned about economic survival through economic good times and bad. Don't leave the development of trust to chance. Don't be satisfied with the situation where you have some staff you trust and others you do not trust. Look at the everyday events as opportunities to teach the development of trust to your employees.

For Discussion

1. What are your strengths and weaknesses? Do you discuss them openly with co-workers? What do you need from colleagues to be successful? What is an example of a way in which you can contribute to the success of others? What structures, biases, values, procedures make it difficult or easy for you to work successfully with colleagues in your organization?

2. How do you feel about sharing your personal experiences with co-workers? What might be the benefits of doing so? What boundaries do you need to have in order to feel comfortable?

3. How would you evaluate the trust level in your organization? If you can trust each other more, how will it strengthen the work you do?

4. What has happened to you on the job which made you trust your co-workers or your organization as a whole, more...or less? What are some real-life examples of the importance of trust on the job?

NOTES

eight

Make Respect a Part of Your Culture

**"I firmly believe that respect is a lot more
important, and a lot greater, than popularity."
-Julius Erving**

It's hard to think about RESPECT without the strains of Aretha Franklin's great hit R-E-S-P-E-C-T ringing in your ears. It's almost like the word belongs to her. But the word also gets lots of use when we are talking about employee morale. A recent post in a LinkedIn group asked the question…"What can supervisors do to prevent social workers from burning out?" The flood of answers to that question was amazing. But the word that kept coming up was, you guessed it, **respect**. Evidently there's frequently a real lack of respect between management and line social service workers. Some expressed gratitude for the relationship they had with their boss too, but the overwhelming majority had a bad relationship with their boss and cited a lack of respect as one of the frequent causes. Many were prepared to leave if another opportunity became available. They thought highly of the mission of the organization they worked for but their supervisor was the cause of much disappointment and anxiety. As has been said before by others, "staff don't leave organizations, they leave supervisors."

This is not uncommon. Social workers and lots of others too, will complain about a lack of respect that they sense from their boss. So the word is used a lot. What does it mean? What management behaviors define respect? Do we recognize respectful behaviors when we see them? Here are seven management behaviors which illustrate an attitude of respect for line employees.

1. *Managers allow input into decisions that effect staff.* Simply put, management holds the work done by staff in high regard. They believe that staff, based on their everyday work have, or should have, a valid opinion about problems facing the organization and they want to incorporate those views into whatever decision they ultimately make. The staff recommendation may or may not be similar to the decision the boss eventually makes. Usually people do not insist on having their own way; they just appreciate the opportunity to have their views heard. Being listened to sends the message that they are respected.

2. *Managers go out of their way to form positive relationships with staff.* Forming good relationships at work is not a different process from that which we experience in our personal lives. When we want to have a positive relationship with someone, we go out of our way to try to help them; we show concern when they are in pain of some kind and we celebrate with them in times of success. We share their interests. This means that supervisors and managers laugh with staff during the good times and cry with them during the bad times. They demonstrate that the feelings staff have about how things are going are legitimate and "okay". They find out what the interests of staff are; they find out what they get excited about during non-work hours. Over time, they learn about the personal battles that staff have had to fight in order to be where they are today. All of this they do without being unprofessional or without prying for information. But when it happens, the

bond between manager and staff becomes immeasurably stronger.

3. *Managers learn from mistakes; they don't blame or find fault.* It's easy to point the finger of suspicion and blame at a low-paid employee when something goes wrong. A respectful relationship between management and line staff is built when managers focus more on learning from a mistake than they focus on finding out who messed up and assigning suitable punishment. There is more about this in Chapter 14 on Accountability but we need to remember that blame and learning are like oil and water...they don't mix well with each other. When we find one employee or a small group of employees to blame for a mistake, the organization will normally not have learned very much from the problem which resulted.

4. *Managers recognize when work loads are heavy or when an exceptionally difficult task has been accomplished.* Give staff the guidance they need to set priorities so they can leave work every day with a feeling of accomplishment. Acknowledge when a difficult task has been completed and done in exemplary fashion. Say "thank you, nice job." I have never heard a staff member say, "my boss compliments me too often." Rather what I am accustomed to hearing is that "my boss only talks to me when I have made a mistake." Set a goal for yourself to say "thank you, nice job" three times each day. Don't say it insincerely. Make it mean something. Be on the lookout for people doing a good job.

5. *Managers use humor to help people relax.* There is always a humorous side to every situation. Help people see it; point it out. In my life, I have always felt more relaxed and competent when someone has laughed with me about the jam I was in. I've always been grateful for that and your staff will be too. There is usually a humorous side to everything that happens, but we overlook it because

of our feelings of anger, guilt, shame, or inadequacy. In today's internet age, believe it or not, there are websites that routinely carry jokes for social workers and about social workers. For example, www.friedsocialworker.com or http://www.communitycare.co.uk.

6. ***Managers are teachers, not cops***. This means that you are spending your time helping people learn, not trying to capture them making a mistake. Adults learn differently than do children and as a manager, you need to become an expert adult educator. Good teachers are committed to the success of their students; your employees will love that you are in "their corner." In social services we say we know how to help our clients grow and develop. Our staff can learn just like our clients do. Being a good teacher of adults means that we have done an assessment of the strengths and weaknesses of every staff member and have outlined a set of procedures designed to help staff learn a new task. Finally we monitor their performance and give them constructive feedback. We're investing a lot of time and effort in their development because we **respect** them and their potential.

7. **As a supervisor, listen to your employees**. Other chapters in this book have great tips for people who want to develop good listening skills. Listening is hard work and requires a tremendous amount of physical and psychological focus; but it definitely demonstrates your respect.

Things are never going to be perfect. We will often have to work under less than ideal conditions. But as author and philosopher Charles Swindoll said, life is 10% what happens to you and 90% what you do about it. Let's stay positive. Respect each other!

For Discussion

1. Have you ever had a boss that complemented you every day or at least several times a week? How did that leave you feeling?
2. In your experience, which supervisors did you admire the most? Which ones taught you the most and how did they do it?
3. Sometimes supervisors and managers are disrespectful without realizing it. Give some examples of when you have seen this happen.
4. What happens to staff teams where the manager sits in his office all day and does paperwork?
5. Think about one of your staff members specifically. What is your plan to take that person from his/her current level of performance to a higher level...to learn a new task?

NOTES

nine

Provide Job Security

"Strong managers who make tough decisions to cut jobs provide the only true job security in today's world. Weak managers are the problem. Weak managers destroy jobs."
-Jack Welch

Have you ever been laid off? It happened to me in the mid-1980s. I thought I saw a chance, for the first time in my life to earn a lot of money, and I made the leap from the not-for-profit world to for-profit operations. It lasted about six months. Then the owner came to my desk one afternoon and said, "Larry, I can't afford you anymore." It was a devastating wake-up call. He was a new owner and there were many things that he needed to learn from me about the building we occupied. I had successfully taught him everything he needed to know and now he no longer needed me or my salary. I went home and nervously told my wife the unexpected news. Fortunately she was securely employed and after a few months I was again employed. So it all turned out ok but it was a hard lesson…now more than ever, it can happen to anyone.

Surveys about factors which create job satisfaction have repeatedly identified the following factors as being the most important: challenging work, recognition, input into what affects their job,

job security and promotional and growth opportunities. This chapter explores the importance of providing job security.

Job security is especially important when unemployment in the general population is high. Right now, job security is certainly an issue for almost every American worker. Everyone is anxious to complete another week without having received a lay-off notice. Announced job loss numbers can from time to time be staggering; this depressing information has been a part of the evening news shows for most of the last several years. What's not so new is that the work force has had the feeling that management feels no sense of responsibility to maintain their jobs.

Since the 1950's, American industry has treated employees as pawns in a magnificent chess game. Employees were relocated across the country, from one company facility to the other, without sensitivity to the havoc brought to families of those affected. Gone are the days when you worked for one company in one location until retirement. Gone are the days of company-provided housing. With several rare exceptions, employers today are looking for ways to lower their commitment to employees and the corresponding costs.

Traditionally in the non-profit world, things have been more stable and only recently have we seen human service organizations involved in lay-offs. One New Jersey welfare office recently downsized from 90 social workers to 60. That's a huge cut and adds another layer of stress on top of an already very stressful work situation. It is a strange experience for social workers and others who for years have enjoyed job security and good benefits at the cost of a lower salary.

Throughout the American work force, employees lack a sense of loyalty to the company and do not feel engaged with the larger mission and objectives of the company; it is merely a reflection of the apparent lack of loyalty and engagement that management has felt toward the workforce over the years. I believe this is a stereotypical view that employees have of management. In order to change this, every company and organization will need to have a specific plan to demonstrate their commitment to high levels of worker satisfaction and retention. This will need to be reinforced with day to day management decisions which are aligned with their stated commitment.

What can employers do to demonstrate their commitment to providing job security for their workers, even in these troubling economic times? Here are nine simple, mostly no -cost steps, you can and should take.

1. Be honest. If you are in financial trouble, make sure that employees know that and also know what they can do to help. It's critical that what you say is credible.
2. Involve employees in the solution. Sometimes their solutions may be better, more realistic and more helpful, than what you had in mind. They know where money can be saved. You've no doubt heard about companies where employees got together and decided to take one furlough day a month to avoid layoffs.
3. Listen to staff in both formal and informal settings. Take action on their suggestions whenever possible or explain why you are not able to implement an idea. As I have stated in the previous chapter, most people do not insist on having their suggestion implemented, but they will feel better about a decision you made if they sense that you really listened and considered their idea.
4. Be smart about hiring. If a layoff is on the horizon, eliminate existing vacancies whenever possible. Make good hire decisions. Hiring people who fit with your needs and expectations is especially important. Be careful about short-term, grant-funded positions. If new, grant-funded hires are always laid off when the grant runs out, each

time that happens, a shock wave of distrust rolls through the organization. Everyone, even those in "permanent" positions begin to wonder, "am I next?" Organizations that are growing will frequently be able to absorb employees from grant-funded positions into more permanent parts of their service system.

5. Invest in training so that you get the most out of every person you have. In hard economic times, training may be the very first thing eliminated. On the whole, it should be the last. When times are tough, you need everyone to be at their best in terms of performance. Choose training experiences wisely, however, and continue training on topics where there can be a big return on the investment. There are very inexpensive ways to have an active training program – also see Chapter 20. Sometimes you can use in-house talent to do the training. This may not always be appropriate but it's a way to continue training and at the same time, recognize employees with particular talent and experience. Seemingly every day there are new resources on the internet which are available free or for a minimal charge.

6. Be positive. Acknowledge good work and illustrate how quality affects organizational cost-effectiveness. Get employees focused on outcomes; not anxious about possible coming lay-offs. It's always important that you, as the leader, are highly visible during difficult times. Don't hide in your office, get out there and communicate, in fact, over-communicate with staff. Show a willingness, even a desire to hear and respond to even the most difficult of questions.

7. Anticipate budget problems early on – the earlier remedial steps are taken to correct a shortfall, the less negative impact on staff and program.

8. Know what the cost of employee turnover is. Generally turnover costs fall into two categories. First there is the

direct cash expense: advertising and recruiting, interviewing, background checks, physicals, orientation and training, financial implications on unemployment, workers compensation and other benefit costs. That category can easily be $1000 or more per turnover incident. Secondly there are the non-cash or indirect costs of turnover. Like reduced staff morale;, lost expansion opportunities, the loss of organizational knowledge, an increase in` mistakes that new employees often make. This category, the indirect costs of turnover can actually be significantly more expensive than the direct or cash costs. When you understand how much turnover, in total, costs your organizations, you can intelligently decide how much to spend on reducing turnover thorough training, increased benefits etc.

9. Remember, employees who stay with you during hard times are not necessarily happy; they may just be waiting for the economy to pick up so they can profitably "jump ship". In hard times, do everything you can possibly do to keep employees happy and engaged; you'll never regret that investment, and you'll be ready for the next growth opportunity that comes along. Until you have identified the cost of turnover however, any preventative measures will seem too expensive.

10. As I look around, I think it's fair to say that the organizations who have been able to avoid layoffs in the past five years are the ones who are proactive. Always developing talent, always looking at expansion opportunities, always looking for efficiencies, at doing things better and faster. Waiting till the money gets tight is too late. At that point, part of your psyche is going to be immersed in fear and pessimism and the decisions you make will, because of that, likely be flawed.

A real test of leadership is when employee jobs are at stake. As mentioned earlier it is a time to maximize opportunities for leaders to communicate. Helping everyone to see the preventive measures being taken to avoid lay-offs; the organization's history of handling difficult situations; and what things will be like when the crisis has been avoided are key messages to make sure everyone hears. Having this information will help everyone remain committed to the tasks at hand and lend a comfortable feeling of normalcy and stability to the organization.

For Discussion

1. Have you ever been laid off? What things helped you get through this experience successfully?
2. What was the last major crisis (of any kind) faced by your organization? What lessons can be learned from how that was handled?
3. How comfortable are you operating in an environment of transparency so that all employees have the opportunity to learn about the organization's challenges?
4. What strengths does the organization have that can be leveraged during times of uncertainty and potential crisis?
5. When money is tight, in what specific ways can middle managers and front line supervisors be of particular help?

NOTES

ten

Give 'Em a Hug

**"There is a real danger that computers will develop
intelligence and take over. We urgently need to develop
direct connections to the brain so that computers can add
to human intelligence rather than be in opposition."**
-Stephen Hawking

Recently the American Academy of Pediatrics has issued a warning that stress can harm children for life. The warning is based on 20 years of research. To children, alcohol, drugs, abuse, neglect, homelessness are all threatening and traumatizing. And, the result is that these children are statistically more likely to develop heart disease, obesity, diabetes and other physical ailments as adults. They are also more likely to struggle in school, have short tempers, have problematic interpersonal relationships, and have run-ins with law enforcement.

The interesting thing is that some very simple changes can make a big difference. For example the study found that when parents received visits from a pediatric nurse from before childbirth to the child's second birthday, it's great for their children. By the time those children are 15, they are only 1/3 as likely to have behavioral or cognitive problems, and their arrest records are half as great as children whose parents did not receive the support. The visiting nurses carried no magic wands, just warned parents of the dangers of substance abuse, and encouraged them to read to their children and to cuddle them as often as possible. Not revolutionary techniques, but actions that make a difference.

This research, which illustrates the impact that small interventions can make, started me wondering about the impact of a supportive environment on the children and adults that many of us have in care and about the impact of a supportive environment on the caregivers: youth workers, house parents, aides, direct support professionals. What we all **believe** to be true, is in fact, true: when caregivers feel supported, the care they give is quantitatively and qualitatively better and the probable outcomes for those receiving care are improved. Human beings want connection. They need to feel that others care about them and what they do.

We are living and working in an era of high pressure. There is little money for pay raises, for special activities; for anything. During the recent holiday season, some employees had to pay to attend their own party. Everyone has to be focused all the time; no time to relax and reflect. The emphasis is on paperwork and doing more with fewer resources.

Our relationships are electronic, even at work. We stay in touch with friends and co-workers via email and texting. Yet, since we are human, as the research around at-risk children demonstrates, we need more direct human contact than that in order to thrive. We need someone to check in with us...find out how we are doing. We need a hug once in a while, not just a noisy cell phone to remind us that there are people out there who want to connect with us. Yes, there have been times when a phone call made a big difference to me. But there have been more times when I have been positively affected by a touch, a smile, eye contact which said, "I care about you" or "I understand". These seem to be very basic human needs and as human service leaders we have an important role to play in making sure that our employees have these needs met. Pay attention to your employees. Spend time with them. Listen. It's that simple.

This is not an anti-technology rant. It is a plea for social service agencies, in the midst of all the stress and pressure, to make sure that you are helping staff feel more needed and worthwhile. Staff want a sense that they are connected to the mission of your organization. They want to know their ideas are heard, that their good work is always acknowledged. They will feel more human, more alive and more worthwhile and will pass that along to those you are trying to serve.

The move from campus-based services to community services has also contributed to a sense of isolation and aloneness amongst human service employees. Now the typical scenario, even in large organizations, is for employees to be assigned to a small site, sometimes at great distance from the corporate headquarters. Or, they work out of their cars, going from one client to the next...mobile therapists. It's a wonderful thing most of the time, but it does isolate people from support, from role models, from supervision. If you manage a "mobile therapist", find time to connect with them. If need be, go on the road with them. Make sure they understand that you are not there to second guess them or to look over their shoulder. You are there to listen and understand. Your verbal and non-verbal behavior can clearly establish the difference.

Your staff are up against some incredible challenges. Your job as a manager is to give them a reason to keep trying. I once described it as being a "broker of hope." Your personal presence can help people keep trying. You'll be amazed at the job they will do. It's a small thing but it can make a big difference.

For Discussion

1. Do your employees feel isolated and at the same time pressured? Is it "sink or swim" for your people?
2. Do you have a standard of supervision frequency as an organization?
3. What procedures do you have in place to encourage employees to stay in touch with each other? Have you been able to use technology to help with this? How do new employees learn to know colleagues?
4. How does your organization distribute praise and acknowledge good work?
5. Are supervisors evaluated based on their ability to support their employees?
6. Have you had training in becoming a better listener or in how to use body language to convey support and encouragement?

NOTES

eleven

Discover Employee Dreams

**"The vision that you glorify in your mind, the ideal
that you enthrone in your heart – this you will
build your life by, and this you will become."**
-James Allen

Several years ago, a coach I had hired asked me to list what my dreams were. What did I hope or wish for: for myself, for my family, for my company, for people who were important to me. After a week, I had a list of 12 or so down on paper. I shared the list with him and he said, "Keep listing them; you're not trying hard enough." Sure enough in the next few days, I added another 24. They came in fits and starts and at all times of the day and night. They would wake me up at night; they happened in the shower, over my morning coffee, when I was dead tired at night. They came from childhood, from thoughts and hopes I had as a younger man. The point is that dreams, new ideas, new hopes and wishes can be cultivated and the more cultivation we do, the more dreams will surface. The other lesson I learned is that our dreams don't die all that easily. A dream you had as a child is still with you, even if you have not thought about it in many years.

Every major accomplishment in the world today began in someone's head. It began as a dream. Do you pay attention to your dreams and to the dreams of your staff? If not, you could be missing out on some really amazing ideas. We need to value dreams more. Because we are all different people from birth, our ideas...our dreams contain different insight into the world around us. Think about the great discoveries in science, and technology; airplanes; electricity; light bulb; complex medical procedures; the computer; cell phones. These things did not just appear one day. They started out in someone's mind – maybe at the end of a long day, or during the night or first thing in the morning. The thought occurred to them, "I wonder if..."

Everyone has dreams; dreams of how their lives and the lives of those around us could be better. For some the dreams may be few and far between; no one has asked them about their dreams in a long time and so they have stopped paying attention. Too many people have told them, "you've gotta be realistic; stop trying." Usually when our dreams are "realistic", they look very similar to what goes on in our every day life right now. We will achieve no more than that to which we have become accustomed.

To those who are listening and paying attention, dreams are the drivers of innovation. Sometimes they are insignificant with no particular message or direction. Other dreams are frequent, life changing, and profound.

Employees have ideas...have hopes that organizations could be more effective and better places to work. Ask them to share their thoughts often. You never know when someone might share something that could give you a totally different slant on the challenges you have been struggling with.

If your only concern is that employees put in 8 hours of honest work, you are only getting half a loaf from them. Their hopes, ideas and dreams may represent their most powerful contribution to the organization. But paying attention to dreams requires a special kind of freedom that few give themselves or those around them. Dreamers, people who come up with exciting, out of the box ideas, are often criticized. The really good ones however, are not deterred by criticism. Consider, for example:

- Henry Ford was told that what people really wanted was a faster horse.
- Alexander Graham Bell was told that the telephone had too many flaws to ever be taken seriously.
- Thomas Edison failed miserably, hundreds of time, before he could get a light bulb to ignite; once he caused an explosion in his lab.
- The Wright Brothers were told that a heavier than air machine would never fly.
- Michael DeBakey's first few heart transplant patients all died within a few hours of surgery; now we do 10-15 successful heart transplants a day in this country and recipients live for many years with an excellent life quality.

Imagine the cost to society if these persons would have abandoned their dreams in the face of failure. Imagine Martin Luther King saying, "I have a dream...but I don't think they are ready for it yet."

So are you really mining your employees for their ideas about how to make things better: more effective, more efficient? Here are four tips from Alex Osborn that will help you motivate your staff to share their ideas:

1. Defer judgment. No criticism of anyone's idea. Don't be a "wet blanket".
2. Strive for quantity. The more ideas you come up with the more likely that one or more of them will be a game-changer.

3. Encourage the really weird or crazy ideas. The wilder, the better. Osborn said, "It's easier to tame down than it is to think up."

4. Look for opportunities to link ideas together and create something more powerful than either one of them would have been separately.

Theodore Roosevelt at the Sorbonne in 1910 said that "…the critics and naysayers, the nags and the negative people in our lives who want to tell us, 'No. It can't be done. Don't try. Give up. Why do you have to stand out? Why don't you just be sensible and give in to the inevitable?' Don't buy into their message of settle-settle, underachievement and muddle-along now." Pay attention and dare to live your dreams…at work too.

Some employers have recently established the position of Dream Manager. The employee is responsible to help other employees articulate and realize their personal dreams. No, there is not a lot of money to be given away, but the Dream Manager can help employees learn about community resources of which they were not previously aware. The Dream Manager can also help the employee establish and structure a short or long range plan that eventually enables the employee to realize his or her dream.

Can't afford a Dream Manager you say? Well, that could be a problem, but on the other hand if establishing the position could help you reduce turnover, then some costs would be offset by establishing this interesting fringe benefit.

Your organization needs new ideas. The world is changing too fast for us to be certain that yesterday's solutions will be helpful. But as the leader, you don't have to come up with all of them yourself. In fact, your primary job is to get them from your staff. Extend to your employees the power of being the drivers of your success. Dream on! Dream on!

For Discussion

1. What do you think your organization will look like in 10 years? Who will you be serving? What services will you be providing? What products will you bring to market?
2. Who amongst your employees would you call a "dreamer". Are you paying any attention to that person? Why or why not?
3. What do you think your organization could do to encourage creativity and innovation amongst your employees?
4. Does your organization even need, or could they benefit from, innovation right now?
5. What one "dream" would you like to see become real in the next 12 months?

NOTES

twelve

Preserve the Family Ties of Employees

"A mother's love for her child is like nothing else in the world. It knows no awe, no pity, it dares all things and crushes down remorselessly all that stands in its path."
-Agatha Christie

Psychologists call it *spillover;* when one area of life "spills over" into another. So it is that what happens at work impacts our family life. Kevin Kruse discusses how when things are going bad at work, it negatively impacts our health, our relationships, the behavior of our children, our overall happiness and quality of life. And he cites research to buttress his assertion. Kevin says, "Working for a bad boss may be as harmful to your heart as smoking." If you have ever hollered at your wife, children or pet after a bad day at work, you know about spill over.

Not too long ago, a friend of mine told me about how aggravated her daughter was when a group home manager called my friend at 10:00 in the evening. The daughter really felt like her time with her mom had been interrupted by a phone call from work. And so it goes with many of us who have had management positions in human services or in other fields for that matter. Our work is never done and there is never enough time to do everything. Our workplace culture, values arriving early and working late. Yet if we are to be really satisfied on the job, our family life must be satisfying as well; the two are tied together. Today the issue is not so much work-life balance but work-life blend.

Looking at workplace satisfaction numbers gathered by the Gallup organization over the last 10 years, one can see a marked decrease in the level of satisfaction of American workers. This situation should seriously concern us all. How do I make sure that the mission is accomplished and still make sure that employees are giving their personal lives and their families the attention that each deserves? There are important times that families should be together and if employers do not take that into consideration, everyone loses. Over the years, I have heard many parents say that they won't do this or that when asked by their supervisor because "my kids are the most important thing to me...not this job". On the surface, the comment can sound insubordinate and I can easily imagine that it probably cost more than a few people their job. Now whether or not the parent actually was fired for being insubordinate, I cannot say, and it's not the real point anyway. What is important for employers is that the parent-child tie is a strong one and in most cases society is better because of it. Smart employers will do everything possible to avoid a situation where an employee has to choose between the job and the child. This is not easy to accomplish, especially in 24 hour care situations, but a supervisor who recognizes and respects parental responsibility will engender tremendous respect and loyalty from employees.

Here are six suggestions that will help you be a family-friendly employer:

1. Be clear about priorities - Understand what things are most important to each and every employee. Write them down for future reference. To accomplish this, honest discussion and listening must happen. And, it's not a

once-and-done situation. Things change and it's your job to make sure your understanding of employee priorities is important. Don't forget, everyone's situation and priorities are different.

2. As much as it is reasonable, make it possible for employees to structure their life so that it reflects their priorities. This is not easy. It will be especially difficult for employees who travel or for staff who help provide 24 hour coverage. In these situations there can easily be a clash with the expectations of the employee's family. But, managers are paid for creativity too.

3. Seek the support of others - As you attempt to live by your priorities, seek the counsel and support of other leaders. Find out how other organizations are helping employees to maintain a healthy work-family balance or blend; you may also get wise counsel from within your own organization.

4. Be realistic about your schedule and commitments - Don't over commit in terms of your own schedule and don't allow employees to do it either. Make sure that you can keep the promises you make. .

5. Make family-work blend a topic of regular staff discussion, especially with other leaders. Don't wait until there's an emergency situation or a major conflict to discuss it.

6. Develop recommendations for employees to help them address the push and pull of work and personal life. When you are preparing these recommendations, solicit employee input. It is always a good idea to request input from the people most likely to be effected. Plus, buy-in or compliance is more likely to occur if employees feel like their views have truly been heard. Distribute these recommendations and/or post them for all to see. Encourage work teams to discuss them – it's a good use of company time. Those recommendations might include things like:

- <u>Wherever you are</u> - Be present, not only physically but psychologically and emotionally. Pay attention to those around you.
- <u>Get enough sleep and exercise</u> - Managing the demands of your life requires judgment and energy. Be well equipped for this with a good night's sleep.
- <u>Recognize that you have limitations and cannot do it all</u> - Sometimes others will have expectations for you that you simply cannot meet. Of course it depends, but it's often ok to say "no".
- <u>Learn to delegate</u> - Identify, at work and at home, the tasks that only you can do. Get help with the rest.
- <u>Prioritize and use your time well</u> - There is always enough time to do the most important things.
- <u>Give everyone input</u> whose life is impacted by your decisions: family, friends, co-workers.

There are some really hard decisions to be made sometimes in the area of work-family blend. Conclusions may be different for each organization and for that matter, each person. Active and frequent discussion will surface the best ideas to resolve these conflicts.

For Discussion

1. Since the answers to this dilemma are often very individual, what have you found to be an effective tool for balancing your work and personal life?
2. Do you think that your organization could benefit from training in managing time and setting priorities? Why or why not?
3. How could things be organized so that we were more efficient in our use of time?
4. What could we do to make our organization more "family friendly"?
5. Role-play a discussion between a supervisor and an entry level employee about the employee's request to be off duty so that he can accompany his wife to their child's 1-year old physical exam. Get feedback from those observing the role-play.

NOTES

thirteen

Recognition – Acknowledge Work Well Done

"Start with good people, lay out the rules, communicate with your employees, motivate them and reward them. If you do all those things effectively, you can't miss."
-Lee Iacocca

When I was in my 40's, my father told me an interesting story which helped me understand him a lot better than I did up to that point. He said that when his older brother began his senior year in high school, their father promised him an air rifle if he got all A's during his last year. This promise was not lost on my father who when he came to his senior year in high school assumed that the same deal held for him. To his surprise, after he had gotten the A's, his father said "performing well is its own reward". So there may well have been some favoritism operating here, but my father was, by his own account, deeply hurt by this misunderstanding with his father. But many people of that era felt that way; that there was no need to acknowledge extra effort or hard work or very excellent work. "It was its own reward."

But now, the not-so-surprising ending to this story. A number of years after I heard this story from my father, one of my direct reports came to me and said, "Larry, I think that you believe I do good work, but you never tell me that." My reticence to provide my staff with the acknowledgement they needed was a lesson I had learned from generations before me. It's perhaps a lesson that many of us need to learn – to be more open and giving regarding our feelings of appreciation. Otherwise, we completely miss opportunities to further develop a positive relationship with our employees...a relationship which yields greater employee commitment and a better quality of day-to-day work.

Recognition is something we all want; it's right in there with the rest of what we often refer to as common human needs. Earlier I commented, "I have never heard someone say 'my boss compliments me too much.'" On the contrary, I have heard many employees say that the only time they hear from their supervisor is when they have done something wrong. When this happens, the divide between employees and supervisor will do nothing but grow wider. I used to work for someone who would approach you every morning, and within the first five minutes that he was talking with you, he would find five or six positive things to say to you. He might have been commenting on some work you had finished or he might have been talking about the shirt you were wearing. He was an imperfect man in some other respects, but he was very skilled at paying attention to his employees and because of that he had tremendous influence with them. He was their leader, about that there was no debate.

Recognition can be given in public or in private. In fact, giving praise and recognition should be done in both public and in private settings; each setting provides its own unique and important benefit. My teenaged daughter recently received public recognition in the school newspaper for an achievement. However, for the same achievement, she received a letter sent to our home, addressed to her, from the school principal. Both made her eyes light up with pride...and her father's too.

Recognition leads to pride in the workplace; a positive feeling about being affiliated with a company, organization or an individual manager. It can begin before employment even starts. In another chapter of this book we discuss *on-boarding*, a relatively recent talent management technique which attempts to help new employees develop an immediate positive identification with the new employer.

There are six other important ways that recognition can be used to develop employee pride and loyalty.

1. All employees should have the opportunity to interact with the chief executive of the company. This should happen as soon as possible after hire. This can begin with a photo opportunity during the first week of employment. How great it would be if the picture of the new employee standing alongside the CEO would be published in the local paper; you can count on this newspaper issue to make its way around the new employee's family and friends.

2. Every employee needs to hear how his or her job relates to the overall success of the company. No one can do this more effectively and with greater impact than the person in charge of the organization. And because the CEO took the time to speak personally to an employee leads that employee to conclude that he or she is an important part of the company's success.

3. Supervision can be done in a way that adds to the feelings of importance that an employee has. When the supervisor takes phone calls or allows others to interrupt the supervisory conference, it does not add to the employee's feelings of worth.

4. Supervisors must be looking for employee success that they can build upon. Too often supervisors see their role as watching to catch an employee making a mistake so that

they can point that out to them, write them up or take even more severe disciplinary action. Try to catch employees doing something right and acknowledge their good work. You can't do it too often. As a supervisor, put yourself on a quota of giving out at least five compliments each day.

5. Establish a minimum supervisory contact level for every employee. Supervision is not done by simply saying "hello" as you pass your direct reports in the hallway. Supervision should be done in a quiet, safe environment where the employee's privacy is protected. The discussion should include a review of the employee's performance, not just a coordination of activities and schedules. The performance discussion should be done regularly and not saved up for the annual performance review. If as a supervisor, you are having conferences with your employees at least once a month, you are providing supervision at a bare minimum satisfactory level. It all depends on the employee, but many will benefit from contact which is more frequent than that. Too often we think of supervision as being for the purpose of correcting performance problems. Good supervision really is about the growth and learning of the employee. It has a very positive emphasis. If nothing else, it communicates to the employee that at least for that supervisory hour, they are the most important person in the organization.

6. Finally, don't overlook the time spent in informal contacts. Informal training is a hot concept right now in the Human Resources field. So while I earlier noted that passing in the hallway does not constitute supervision, those occasions are nonetheless opportunities to further cement the employee's positive feelings about being involved with the company and deepen their pride at being connected with the team. The same dynamic operates when supervisors interact with employees in informal, non-work settings.

You would think that most human service organizations would understand this pretty well and implementation of some of these techniques would come very naturally to them; after all, they are in the people business. We know what it takes for a client to achieve new goals – we can help them get from Point A to Point B. But when it comes to our employees, we believe that all we should have to do is tell them what to do and it's their job to figure out how to do it. But we can change that if we are determined to do so. The payoff for doing so is employees who are happy, loyal and productive.

For Discussion

1. What are the standards for good supervision at your organization?
2. Do employees emerge from supervision feeling better or worse about their work?
3. How and under what circumstances do supervisors and their employees have contact with each other?
4. As a supervisor, how long has it been since you have received a compliment for your work? How long has it been since you gave a compliment?
5. Does your organization give more time and attention to employee mistakes or to excellent work? How did this feature of your culture develop and what maintains it?
6. What are three things that could be done at your organization to recognize employees for their good work?

NOTES

fourteen

Develop a Culture of Accountability

"A body of men holding themselves accountable to nobody ought not to be trusted by anybody."
-Thomas Paine

What is accountability? Accountability refers to character and integrity. It has to do with your ability and willingness to do what you promised you would do. To follow through according to an agreement, direct or implied. Actually, accountability occurs at three levels. First it is what we do individually. This can include behavior where no one else is directly involved. For example, I promise myself that I am going to lose weight. Whether or not I actually do lose weight is a measure of my accountability...even if only to myself. Secondly, there is accountability which is interpersonal. We promise a colleague that we will finish a report before the end of the week. Again, how we handle this commitment is a measure of our accountability. Third, is organizational accountability. If the organization communicates to an employee or a group of employees that they will be receiving a salary increase, but then the increase doesn't happen, there is a breach of accountability.

There are lots of examples where individuals, groups of employees and organizations suffer from a lack of accountability.

In its mildest form, a lack of accountability is illustrated by employees who do the absolute minimum to get by and who fail to follow established procedure unless their behavior is directly monitored by a superior. When there is no accountability, employees look for loopholes in supervision or procedure which allow them to perform below an acceptable level. In more serious forms, a lack of accountability is present when employees are more deliberate in violating policy or supervisory expectation. In these situations employees seem not to care whether or not their behavior is noticed. They are only driven by their own agenda; what they feel like doing. In the final analysis, an organization's lack of accountability results in lost opportunity, decreased production, poor morale and high turnover. Other accountability-related issues are discussed in Chapter 6 entitled Stop the Blame Game.

Up to this point, you might assume that the measure of accountability is only applied to those at the bottom of the organizational ladder. Actually, to be successful and sustainable, everyone from top to bottom must be accountable. In fact, accountability must be an identifiable feature of the organization's culture. You should be able to see it in operation.

Employees at all levels can act like they are not accountable for their actions. It's not just the lower level staff who sometimes gets by with behavior which is below known expectations. Supervisors and managers who don't follow through on promises are yet another illustration of a lack of accountability. Many supervisors, according to most surveys, are not trusted by their direct reports. For example, a University of Florida study indicated that nearly half of all employees did not expect that their supervisors were willing to be accountable for their own behavior.

Do you have a culture of accountability in your organization? If your answer is "no", you are not alone. Most of us know organizations where there are, at best, accountability lapses. For example, I was to present a workshop to a group of 35 supervisors at a well-known NJ rehabilitation center. When I arrived and the workshop actually began, only 18 people were present. One or two straggled in during the presentation. But that was it. Someone had not followed through and had neglected to inform all the people who were supposed to be attending. Or, about half the group simply decided they were not attending. Had this been the 2nd or 3rd class, I would say they were tired of me. But at the point I began, they had no experience with me, good or bad.

Your organization can begin to develop a culture of accountability by committing to at least one of the strategies outlined below. Implementing even one strategy will improve your situation.

1. Establish high performance expectations from the first day on the job. This begins with a job description which is accurate, complete and realistic. Don't make excuses or dream up reasons why you should allow a brand new employee to make repeated performance mistakes; you're not doing anyone a favor. Delaying feedback results in a situation which is even more difficult to correct. It's like a cut finger; the prognosis for a quick heal is much better if the wound is cleaned and treated immediately.

2. Model the behavior you want. If you want people to accept more responsibility for their behavior, start by admitting your own mistakes; take responsibility for how you do your own job as a supervisor, manager or director. If you want people to learn new skills, develop your own skills. Make it a priority to attend skill-building activities yourself. Be committed to doing a better job today than you did yesterday. Everyone will notice.

3. Set up Expectation Agreements. These are not job descriptions. Expectation Agreements normally have a

more narrow focus. They simply detail how an employee is going to handle a specific situation in the future. They write down what will be the supervisory response to compliance (might be an incentive) and non-compliance (might be a form of discipline). Specificity is the key to a good Expectation Agreement; use one when verbal feedback has not been successful.

4. Only set up expectations that you can enforce and intend to enforce. A milder consequence for non-compliance which you can enforce is better than a more severe consequence which is enforced inconsistently, or not at all. As a manager, you want your reports to know, without a doubt, that you will do what you say you are going to do.

5. Hire the Right People in the First Place (see Chapter 1); make the job hard to get. The job you are hiring for will seem more worthwhile and desirable if you do a rigorous job of employee selection. You want to look for people who will be responsive to your expectations; who are conscientious, have integrity and capable of working in sync with other employees. These people may not always have the highest skill level in terms of what the job requires. But their temperament will make it highly likely that they can meet your expectations, whether or not you are looking over their shoulder. The skills (what to do, when) of the job can be learned. But if someone's character and temperament (attitudes, habits) pushes them to be continually looking for the loophole which allows them to get by with less, their likely employment success is highly problematic. Herb Kelleher, the founder of Southwest Airlines, says that you should always hire for attitude, passion and motivation. They are the qualities which cannot be taught. Skills on the other hand, can be learned over time.

6. Label mistakes as opportunities for learning. Underline the value of telling the truth and honesty...even when the

news is bad. The truth should always be rewarded and not punished. This requires that the work environment be safe; where sharing mistakes is celebrated and reinforced and not punished. Call it, "a humiliation-free zone".

7. When a commitment cannot be met, make sure that there is honest and straightforward communication about what happened that changed the organization's capacity. When times are difficult, it is especially important for managers to be in constant communication with line staff. Too often, managers tend to hide out in their offices when there is bad news.

8. Ask questions; they help understand what really happened. Without that understanding, learning from a mistake might be very difficult.

9. Make the successful pursuit of goals challenging, but achievable. In other words, be realistic about expectations.

Accountability makes everything work better. Don't ignore the problems which arise due to a lack of accountability; they will increase geometrically. At the same time, this is not a call for a rigid, authoritarian type of leadership. The days when we can control people out of fear are over; they will just wait until we are not around and do what they want. My experience leads me to support the contention of management consultant Edwards Deming that errors are frequently related to systemic issues and not performance problems of the individual. Or certainly in the process of investigating unusual incidents the system process should be reviewed along with an examination of the role of individuals employees involved. Organizations and individual employees must be accountable.

For Discussion

1. How would you describe the level of accountability in your organization? What are some examples of the way in which you would describe it?
2. How could the leadership of your organization more consistently demonstrate the value of accountability?
3. Has a lack of accountability undermined services to your clients and customers?
4. Do employees complain about a lack of accountability?
5. If you were going to write down an Expectation Agreement for yourself, so that you more consistently demonstrate accountability, what would it contain?
6. From the above 9 suggestions, which one(s) are already in place in your organization? Which ones could be readily implemented? Which ones would make the most difference?

NOTES

fifteen

Protect Employees from Compassion Fatigue

"Witness the American ideal: the Self-Made Man. But
there is no such person. If we can stand on our own
two feet, it is because others have raised us up. If, as
adults, we can lay claim to competence and compassion, it only means that other human beings have
been willing and enabled to commit their competence
and compassion to us—through infancy, childhood,
and adolescence, right up to this very moment."
-Urie Bronfenbrenner

We used to think of trauma victims as those returning from the
battlefield or victims of sexual assault or other forms of physical assault. Now we are quite certain that trauma victims include
those who have suffered under a much broader range of human
experience. Homelessness, divorce, loss of a spouse, financial
collapse etc. all create the social and psychic conditions identi-
cal to those found in persons who have suffered in more physical ways: problematic relationships; substance abuse; lack of
emotional control; depression and a range of other behavioral
health symptoms. They come to work social service agencies, victims of their traumatic experiences; they have an "attitude", they
want help immediately, they are confused and disoriented, they
are unable to carry through on simple tasks, they are neglectful

of responsibilities. I am sure that you have seen these symptoms and others on a daily basis.

A further finding is that persons who provide help and support to trauma victims, hour after hour, day after day, can easily become victims of trauma themselves. They can readily exhibit some of the same symptoms as those they are servicing plus the quality of their services begins to diminish. They start to sense professional failure and frustration, ommonly called "burn-out". It's just like a communicable disease; you contract it from exposure unless preventative measures are taken.

But the good news is that employees can be protected from this, through their own measures of self-care and also from preventative steps taken by their supervisors and managers. Employees are not protected from compassion fatigue by rubber gloves or cell phones, although they are needed hardware at times. What employees need is a collection of emotional support tools which will protect them from the occupational hazard of compassion fatigue. Just by virtue of proximity to persons in pain, whose lives are characterized by turmoil and desperation, social service workers are prone to become victims. The experience is tiring and eventually leads to "compassion fatigue".

Have you ever been in a restaurant and wondered if the cooks in the back got tired of making the same things day after day, night after night. How do they keep themselves fresh and put a platter together, time after time, which makes the guest feel special? People who are helpers get tired too. They get tired of hearing the same reasons for failure; the same descriptions of abuse and neglect; the same excuses; the same accounts of psychological pain and distortion. They get tired of trying to "meet the client where they are"; they get tired of being "understanding" and carving out a realistic plan of action that they suspect the client will not implement. They get tired.

How do you know if any of your employees have contracted compassion fatigue? Here are ten symptoms of the disease.

1. They're afraid to take time off; they appear totally committed to their work and the mission of the organization. In reality they are imprisoned by it.
2. They assume the worst in every situation and they are hostile toward others who do not share their skepticism.
3. They are distrustful and suspicious; when originally they were full of energy and idealism, now they seem to have lost all of that…and ironically they see the change as positive, a sign of growth.
4. They assume that everyone is taking advantage ("using the system"): clients, staff, and their families.
5. They react in a manner which is out of proportion to the confronting issue.
6. They forget _why_ they do their job.
7. Their performance is not what it used to be; they are forgetful, lose track of details.
8. They suffer from sleep disturbances.
9. They are more argumentative, even with people who are emotionally close to them.
10. Their work interferes with social life.

It takes little imagination to see how compassion fatigue could negatively influence on job performance; that's why it is important to provide employees with necessary protection, or we might even refer to it as _immunization_.

How do employers provide immunization from compassion fatigue? What can be done to keep their staff safe? Just like football players who wear shoulder pads and helmets to avoid injury, there are certain responsibilities our employers should exercise in order to make sure that our work environment is safe and as stress-free as possible.

Here are eighteen ideas that illustrate the "protective gear", the immunizations that employees need:

1. Family-friendly policies; minimize the number of times that an employee is forced to chose between the demands of either the employer or the family. As much as possible, arrange things so that the employee can be with his/her family at important times and still meet your expectations as an employer.

2. Fun, every day; make sure that employees have a stress reliever every day. Front line supervisors will have to be onboard with this since they are the ones that will make it happen. Even if it is only a minute or two that allows each employee to take an emotional break from stress.

3. Develop a culture of learning for everyone from top to bottom of the organization. In another chapter (see Chapter 20) we will talk more about this, but everyone in the organization needs to be a learner. Sometimes, it's not the challenge of the workplace that employees need to learn about; it could be that employees can benefit from learning about life challenges. For example, employees might need to learn about nutrition or about money management. Anything which helps them feel that their employer understands their personal needs and is willing to help them cope. One of the most important things that employees will need to learn is how to take care of oneself.

4. Specific job and program expectations should be clear and employees need to understand why their tasks are important to the organization meeting its mission.

5. Everyone needs the opportunity to sit back, take a deep breath and focus on their work...their performance. It's called individual supervision and it is a lot different than conversations you have passing in the hallway. It's when the employee gets the distinct impression that for the

scheduled hour, he/she is the most important person in the organization.

6. Human service organizations, like many in the traditional business community, must be concerned about employee wellness. Companies with wellness programs don't have them to be "nice" to their employees. They have them because they contribute to a healthier bottom line. You can select different options in terms of what it looks like but start a wellness program; begin with a program that doesn't cost you anything. You might even get better health coverage rates by having an employee wellness program and your absenteeism due to illness should decrease. Contract for an Employee Assistance Program; normally on a per employee basis, they are inexpensive. Bring in professional people once a week to provide wellness programs: weight control; smoking cessation; meditation; nutrition counseling. Find a new massage therapist in the community who is trying to start a practice; invite them to come for an hour or two each week to give free chair massages.

7. Designate someone in your HR office as a "dream counselor" and invite employees to come and discuss their hopes and dreams. This can be very encouraging to employees and many times the "dream counselor" will be able to help the employee connect with a community resource that will help them on the road to achieving their dream. (See Chapter 6)

8. Encourage employees to form special interest groups; hobbies; community service.

9. Facilitate employees getting to know each other socially. When employees enjoy each other's company, the employer wins. So encourage an after hours get together. Provide small incentives so that they occur.

10. Communicate with employees. Listen to what they have to say. Share your ideas and concerns with them and hear

their feedback. Most people will not insist that their way is best but they are very reassured when they get the feeling that they have been heard.

11. Employees need a work environment which is clean, attractive, functional and cared for. If even the plants look sad, no employees will stay very long.

12. When employees have a day off, it should really separate them from normal business. Make calling them a truly rare occasion and then only if an emergency situation exists where only their personal input can make a difference.

13. Give employees recognition for a job well done. Do it publicly and privately; both venues serve a distinct purpose and add value to each other which benefits the employees' self concept.

14. Give employees the tools to do the job. Don't make it hard for them to find a tablet or a fresh pencil or a new cartridge for their printer.

15. Celebrate important events; a new grant received; employee birthdays and anniversaries; a client who achieved a significant milestone; graduations; promotions. They are all reasons for celebration.

16. Encourage new ideas by actually giving them a try. If you want employees thinking about how to improve things, set it up so that their ideas are put into practice, at least on a trial basis. Ask an "innovation committee" to sort through suggestions to find the best ideas for implementation.

17. Avoid canceling or even postponing appointments with individual employees. Of course this will need to happen sometimes but when it does, cancel and reschedule yourself rather than do it by email or through an assistant; maximize the amount of personal, face-to-face contact that you have with your employees.

18. There should be an absolute prohibition on abuse and exploitation. This includes all relationships within the organization, staff to staff; client to staff; client to client.

It's also important for employees to assume some measure of responsibility for their own welfare and happiness. After all, sometimes all management can do is provide the tools; it's up to the employee to use them.

Undoubtedly, there are other ideas but this list should get you thinking about what your organization could be doing to prevent "compassion fatigue". Notice, there are no big expenditures of money here. It will cost you some staff time to implement a formal program. But the benefit you will receive from staff who are working with lower stress levels makes the time investment more than worthwhile. A happy staff member is a better, more competent, and more dedicated staff member. Their client work will be drastically improved.

Our employees are not like computers that run at high speed day after day. They must be refueled and "down for maintenance" periodically. If you want high performance, you will find a way to take care of them. Our employees are also not like computers in the sense that the same repair doesn't work for everyone. Finding the tool that helps employees to be high energy and highly enthusiastic about their work might be very much a function of how well you know their individual styles, strengths and temperaments.

For Discussion

1. Have you ever contracted compassion fatigue? What were the symptoms and what did you do about it? What led to your recovery?
2. Do you agree that compassion fatigue impacts your life and relationships outside of work? For example, your relationship with your spouse, companion or children? You have all heard the story about the man who after a fight with the boss, goes home and kicks the dog.
3. How do you think that compassion fatigue negatively impacts the quality of your services?
4. What would be three things your organization could do right away that would not cost any money, but would help employees avoid contracting compassion fatigue?

NOTES

sixteen

Have Productive Staff Meetings

**"The only summit meeting that can succeed
is the one that does not take place."
-Barry Goldwater**

Meetings do not have a good reputation. We often see them as so much talk without any concrete results. Or we see them as boring. But there is good news. Our meetings can become places of action, exciting to the point where we can't wait for the next one.

One time I fell asleep in an important staff meeting. It was very embarrassing and I had to later apologize to my boss about my apparent lack of engagement with what was going on. That was not a highlight of my career but perhaps some of you have also dreaded staff meetings or other meetings of committees, teams or task forces in which you have participated.

Would you describe these meetings as compelling, important, productive, and critical? Or are they boring, pointless, ineffective, frustrating? Most persons unfortunately see their staff meetings as an exercise in frustration. Few decisions are made and the ones that are made are reversed at the following meeting. Members arrive late. Arguments go unresolved, people are unprepared, they last too long, etc. "All talk and no action" is a frequent description of meetings. Sometimes the discussion bears no connection to the realities of the organization; topics discussed do not address the issues that are most upsetting to staff and members leave the meeting without clarity in terms of what the next steps are that need to be taken.

Two major obstacles that we face in having productive staff meetings are (1) a lack of trust in meeting attendees and (2) a fear of conflict. Both of these problems make it impossible to have honest discussions which reflect the real conditions within the organization. People are reluctant to say how they really feel and in addition no one wants to disagree with the Executive Director or other person in attendance with influence and authority.

Here are fourteen action steps you can take to make your staff meetings interesting and productive.

1. Make sure you have the right people there; give everyone time and create a group experience which develops trust. Some meetings might begin with a time of sharing of significant personal or professional achievement or challenge. Participant's individual level of disclosure about personal information will be voluntary but this will help to bind the group together socially. When this happens, people look forward to attendance because they enjoy being around their colleagues. The environment feels safe and comfortable.

2. Give a week's notice and prepare a written agenda for distribution before the meeting. Nothing beats being ready for the meeting. If you lead a meeting which normally lasts an hour, you would not be wrong if you planned to spend two hours in preparation.

3. If you are an attendee at the meeting, you should be going over the agenda and in particular agenda items in which

you are expected to have input. Again, an hour preparing for a one hour meeting is not unreasonable. Preparation might include:

    a. research on topics of concern

    b. a review of the organization's previous attempts to solve the problem

    c. some simple reflection on the pros and cons of issues connected to each agenda item

You should be able to identify what would be a good outcome of each discussion in terms of the needs of the entire organization, not necessarily your personal agenda or the agenda of the department you represent.

4. Begin the meeting on time. If you continue to wait for late arrivals, you will never start on time and in fact you may find yourself starting later and later, wasting the time of those who have arrived on time and inadvertently reinforcing tardiness and punishing punctuality.

5. Encourage full participation; some people will need more encouragement than others. Especially encourage the expression of varied opinions. If there are no varied opinions, chances are someone is not being honest out of insecurity or fear, both of which threaten the usefulness of the meeting. Sometimes groups need to learn about the difference between disagreement over ideas and discussion which feels like a personal attack.

6. Allow sufficient time for discussion. Don't rush decisions. Allow for a full review of the pros and cons of any possible action or decision. Rushing decisions, by not hearing a full review of the issues, sets you up for making a decision which is short-sighted.

7. Decisions can be reached thru a vote or the group can achieve a consensus. If consensus is not reached or if the vote shows the group deeply divided, acknowledge how hard everyone has tried to resolve the issue and suggest that the matter be tabled until the next meeting. This

allows time for informal discussion amongst the members before an actual vote is taken and increases the possibility that the eventual voting outcome will have a broad base of support. The aim is what Patrick Lencioni calls emotional "buy-in" to every decision. That is, the group as a whole must be able to support, even though some may not have initially agreed with the eventual decision. It also means that every member of the group must be able to say, "we decided" and not "they decided". This ability is a measure of emotional support.

8. Sometimes it helps to introduce variation. Instead of always dedicating meetings to the discussion of difficult issues, occasionally set a meeting or two to discuss only inspirational items. Re-energize yourselves. Or, as another variation, meet in a very different location. It could be outside, under a shade tree when the weather is warm. If you can afford it, meet for breakfast at a nearby restaurant. Occasionally an interesting outside speaker might be engaged to encourage stimulating discussion around ideas not normally a part of the agenda. Try walking meetings. Go for a walk in the neighborhood while you talk. This could also prove to be a great community education strategy for your organization.

9. Stay on the subject and adjourn according to schedule. This may seem contradictory to point number 5 above but group members will have other important things that need their attention. In some cases this means that the group will simply have to adjust their expectations in terms of what will be possible to accomplish at any particular meeting. Trying to "shoe-horn" a decision into an allotted time frame sets you up for making a bad decision. Better to pick up the discussion at the next meeting and move things toward consensus and buy-in.

10. Have ground rules and stick to them, although ground rules should be periodically reviewed for usefulness. Make

decisions about how the group will operate. This involves more than just the time of the meeting, who is going to take minutes etc. But also it could include how the group will handle disagreement. How much open conflict and disagreement will be allowed and how can this disagreement be expressed (voice tone, language choice etc). Different groups will have varying comfort levels with loud voice tone, for example. Is off topic discussion or off topic activity (knitting) allowed? So, as you can see, there are a variety of issues to be agreed upon so that the group will have a clear and agreed upon view of how the group can comfortably proceed.

11. Keep and distribute minutes. This is important so that the decisions (or lack thereof) can be easily recalled. Relying on individual memories is risky. In addition, when the words summarizing a discussion are read in black and white, it makes it much easier to see the words that might be causing discomfort and disagreement. In other words, having minutes assists a group in achieving clarity and common understanding. Also, the recorder of minutes for the group, prior to the next official meeting, will have the minutes reviewed by another member of the group, probably the designated leader. This review will guard against the unintentional inclusion of bias or erroneous statements.

12. Dedicate a portion of each meeting to problems, disappointments and failures. See if a way to avoid these events in the future can be determined. Trust me; everyone will pay attention during these discussions. Yes, success needs to be discussed and celebrated, but there may be more to learn from a review of failures and it will serve as a model for the organization. Healthy organizational cultures emphasize and reinforce learning.

13. Allocate time at the end to evaluate the meeting's performance. Thank the group for their hard work.

14. You should have a general structure for each meeting in mind. You may need to have several kinds of meetings: one to check in with others and clear schedules; one to brainstorm or have a free-floating discussion of issues; one to make decisions; and another to evaluate the progress of the entire organization toward meeting its goals and priorities. Almost every sizeable organization faces the same decision-making challenges. So while this may seem like a lot of time in meetings, the issue is whether or not the issues and challenges are being resolved. You can actually develop a cost-per-decision formula. You may have only one meeting a month and because of that the meeting becomes overwhelmed and bogged down with a too large agenda, then your per-decision cost could be pretty high. Whereas more frequent, tightly focused meetings may consume more total hours, but will actually accomplish their respective agenda at a lower per-decision cost. Patrick Lencioni in his recent work on organizational health reviews a structure of meetings and functions which you might find helpful.

Managing meeting attendees is also a big challenge at times. Calling the meeting to order, reviewing the minutes, hearing the committee reports, setting a date for the next meeting and adjourning are all typical steps to be accomplished in running your staff meeting. In between those steps however, the people in attendance can get in the way of getting done what needs to be done. The interesting thing is that regardless of where you are or what the nature of the company or organization is, the same tactics are played out by those in attendance. To expect that your situation is different is to deny some of the basic ingredients of human nature. So the next time you're planning on running a staff meeting, spend some time thinking about how you are going to deal with the following cast of characters, because chances are, they will all be in attendance.

1. Team Players. You wish everyone was like these folks. They are positive in action and motivation; their participation is active and constructive. They listen attentively. They honestly express their opinion when it is requested. Your goal as the meeting leader is to get everyone to act like these attendees…eventually.

2. Politicians. They want everyone to be happy and supportive but they often have a hidden agenda which is related to what they perceive to be good for them rather than the organization as a whole. It's hard for these people to honestly disagree. Try to surface what their real intentions and priorities are. Ask probing questions and keep digging until you get down to their true goal. This might take several meetings.

3. Sneaks. These are the people whose participation varies depending on who is in the room; they will say one thing at one point and the opposite at another. They are sometimes referred to as "back-stabbers". When you ask them a question, make sure you do so in a way which allows little "wiggle room"; questions to them should call for direct, specific answers.

4. Complainers. They are always criticizing and making judgments. To deal with these people, you have to come to the meeting with excess positive energy; otherwise they will wear you down with their critical comments. Complainers don't know the difference between a gripe that you can't do anything about and an issue to which there might be a solution. You can't let them dominate the meeting. Teach them more appropriate behavior by acknowledging them when they are correct and ignoring their whining. Ask them to be specific in their complaints and to go beyond complaining by suggesting solutions.

5. Lawyers. These people love to argue, whether or not they believe in the side of the debate they are promoting. They seem turned on by antagonism. They will try to get

you into an argument regardless of the issue. Don't get involved in this. Sometimes it's best to confront them outside of the meeting and point out the role they are playing. See if you can help them identify a source of their anger and obstructionist temperament.

If you are lucky you may have only one or two of type of persons in your meeting or maybe the Team Players will clearly outnumber the rest. Be prepared, however, to stay on target and keep an optimistic tone.

Your work to make your staff meetings more productive can jump start your campaign for quality improvement through the organization as a whole. Your effort will lead to getting work done, with everyone's input and buy-in. Staff will start looking forward to these meetings and no one will fall asleep.

For Discussion

1. Do you look forward to your staff meetings? Why or why not?
2. How many times in the recent past have group decisions been made based on the needs of individuals at the meeting rather than on the needs of the organization as a whole?
3. Name three things that would improve staff meetings at your organization.
4. How would you evaluate the level of trust amongst staff members attending your meeting?
5. Are there staff members at your meetings who play dysfunctional roles (politicians, lawyers, sneaks, etc) and what are you doing about these individuals?

NOTES

seventeen

Solve Problems Creatively –

Don't Put on Band-Aids

**"A sum can be put right: but only by going back
till you find the error and working it afresh from
that point, never by simply going on."**
-C.S. Lewis

The late, great George Carlin said there were "seven dirty words"
that you could not say on television. Well, there are five forbidden
phrases that you should not be saying in your next staff meeting
if you want to solve problems. It's got nothing to do with proper
behavior, it's got to do with functionality. These phrases lead to
dysfunctional outcomes for you and your organization and they
should not be spoken...by anyone. Here they are:

1. Tried that before;
2. That will not work;
3. But... ;
4. Here's how that will turn out;
5. It's how we've always done it;

Steve Ventura and Eric Harvey, in a little publication called, "Forget it for Success", describe why it is that these five phrases keep us from being good problem solvers.

Tried That Before only means that you tried the idea once before. So what? It might have been the right solution at the wrong time. Maybe it was implemented poorly and a slight adjustment will make all the difference.

That Will Not Work is a self-fulfilling prophecy kind of statement. A negative attitude like this only inspires failure.

But…is almost the same as that will not work. Get rid of 'buts.'

Here's How That Will Turn Out. Now you've become a predictor of the future; might be your day to go do some gambling. How come no one ever says, "That will turn out great"?

It's How We've Always Done It. If your organization is committed to learning and performance improvement, you already know that there is always a better way to do anything. As someone once said, "Keep on doing what you are doing and you will keep on getting what you are getting."

These are all statements that we make from time to time. When we are trying to solve problems, however, these statements are like a bucket of cold water on the groups thinking and discussion. They stop creativity in its tracks. Negativity is a habit and when it flourishes nothing else does.

Set up ground rules for discussion at problem solving meetings. An important one would be that there are no bad ideas and that every contribution is worthwhile. Keep urging people to suspend judgment. When the discussion gets too negative, call a five minute break and ask everyone to refocus on positive outcomes.

Encourage the expression of a wide range of possible ideas and solutions; reinforce people who make really over the top suggestions; this will spur the creativity of others. Let your team know that many breakthroughs started with out-of-the-box, impractical ideas. There will be plenty of time in the fine-tuning stage for identifying glitches and problems. Your most negative people will be very helpful there. These are all tips for what we commonly call "brainstorming" sessions.

Negative people are not always aware of their negativity and the effect they have on people. Before your next meeting, meet with them one-on-one and ask them what is making them so uncomfortable and unable to maintain a positive focus. Set up a performance improvement plan with them so that they are encouraged to become a member of your team that is increasingly oriented toward positive outcomes,

Another thing that a problem-solving effort must guard against is putting band-aids on a problem. Band-aids work for awhile but they are not a long-term solution. This happens when we really haven't taken the time to study the real underlying problem.

Getting to the root of the problem is not always easy. But here are some sequential steps you can take to ensure that you are really going to be able to identify the problem's root cause.

1. Gather data on the history and background of the problem. How often has this happened before and what have we done in the past to solve the problem; have those solutions been effective?
2. List all the relevant factors: facts, assumptions, educated guesses. Be sure that you understand everything that could be impacting on the occurrence of the problem.

3. List all possible courses of action – this is where the brain-storming tips from above will become very helpful. Each possibility will have its own set of advantages and disadvantages. If there is one option with no disadvantages, the solution is very clear.

4. Discuss and analyze the alternative solutions. Solicit the opinion of all stakeholders including people who may not be present for the discussion. Those people need to weigh-in if a proposed problem-solution will impact their day to day performance in any way. Discuss all positive and negative impacts.

5. Prepare a list of conclusions or best possible solutions.

6. Pick the alternative solution with the best chance of success. Be clear about the cost of this option in both financial and non-financial terms. Prepare an implementation timeline. Update anyone with final authority over implementation as to the work that has been done.

7. Prepare a communication plan. How is the recommended solution going to be communicated? Specifically, what will be said about it by whom and to whom? It usually helps to put the message down in writing so that words which might lead to confusion are identified. In some cases, alternative language can be used.

8. Prepare to present and defend your position. There will be opposition to change...always. People need to hear about the process that supports the new course of action, and they need to be reminded of frustrations they have had in the past with the way things used to be addressed.

The process outlined above may seem tedious and laborious. Leaders sometimes assume that they need to have the answers to all problems at their fingertips. Actually the decisions made by a group are most likely superior to those made "on the fly". By following these steps, you avoid spur of the moment decisions which have not been thoroughly analyzed. The decision that can be arrived at quickly and implemented quickly is often not the one that is best for the long haul. This process invests adequate time in studying the problem and analyzing alternative solutions. These steps ensure that a wide variety of options is explored and increases the possibility that there will be greater buy-in when it comes to implementation.

For Discussion

1. How are decisions made in your organization? Who is involved in the decision-making process and who is left out?
2. What issues might appropriately drive decisions to be made by a single individual or a very small group without outside collaboration?
3. Is your organization over the "that will never work" response to new ideas? How did you accomplish that? What difference did it make?
4. What are the factors within your organization which seem to stifle innovation?
5. Can anyone in your organization suggest new ideas? What is the process for dealing with suggestions from lower level staff?
6. Is there a problem in your organization that, if it could be solved, would greatly simplify your professional life? If so, go ahead and work through the 8-step problem solving sequence that is presented above. See how it works. Modify the process as seems called for in your organization. When you are successful, you will have defined an effective model for solving any problem in your organization.

NOTES

eighteen

Communicate Effectively

"A conversation is a dialogue, not a monologue. That's why there are so few good conversations: due to scarcity, two intelligent talkers seldom meet."
-Truman Capoti

Many times I have heard about staff conflicts that have their roots in poor communication. People who don't understand each other or who hear some, but not all, of what the other person had to say. These are people who will usually misinterpret what the other person said. People who were really too busy to listen or allowed distractions to get in the way of good communication. And lastly, when people don't like each other, or for some reason are threatened by each other, these kinds of misunderstandings develop almost automatically.

Many of us grew up professionally on the old fashioned communication model that in essence said, "I told you how that job was supposed to be done and it's your responsibility to do it as I instructed." This model places the responsibility for good communication on the listener. Now we understand that good communication depends on both the speaker and listener making sure they understand each other; they share responsibility for good communication.

Good communication is really hard to accomplish; we underestimate the challenge. We talk all the time, but confuse that with communication. Communication happens when both the sender and the receiver have a shared or common understanding of what is being discussed. Many things can serve as obstacles to good communication: our *perception* of the situation (for example, have I made a mistake that my boss wants to talk to me about); the *relationship* (if it's someone we know well and trust, misunderstandings are less likely); the *mood* we are in (tired and grumpy people miscommunicate more often than not); our *agenda* (are we looking for a promotion from someone we are talking to); and finally, *language and dialect* (are we trying to communicate in a language which is not native to us or does the person we are talking to speak in an accent with which we are unfamiliar.

We have grown to understand the importance of the nonverbal when it comes to communication. Most experts agree that more than 90% of communication is non-verbal. Imagine that! Too bad that in preparing for a tough conversation, we focus our effort on the words we are going to use rather than on the nonverbal behavior; that's where all the action is. We could probably learn a lot from politicians and presentation skill experts who can design non-verbal behavior in order to convey a particular message.

A good place to begin improving communication is with our ability to listen. Many of us have misconceptions about the skill of listening. Here are several for your consideration:

1. Some think that listening is easy and can be done while lounging with your feet up on a stool. In reality, listening requires energy. Really active listeners undergo the same physiological changes as a person jogging. Want to listen actively? Prepare to work.

2. Listening is more than just understanding words. Many times the words a speaker uses can be clarified, modified or even contradicted by non-verbal behavior: eye contact, rate of speech, positioning of hands/legs, nervous fidgeting etc.

3. Our auditory system makes hearing possible. Real listening however is a process which occurs *in one's mind.* In our mind is stored all of our experiences, successes, failures, fears, prejudices etc. and these things serve to filter and define everything we hear and result in the words we hear having meaning. Further, the physiology of hearing (ears) is different than the physiology of really listening (auditory-neuro). Generally listening happens much faster than speaking by a factor of two to three times. This allows for the mind of the listener to wander and be easily distracted.

4. People can tell if you are an active listener, and this can make a real difference to them. If you are not really listening, your body language sooner or later will reveal your lack of attention.

Another dynamic which makes communication messy is *complaining.* Complaints are gripes about individuals and situations that are based on perception. Complaining can become habitual. People can complain dozens of times each day, but they have no intention of trying to fix the situation that they are bothered about. Complaints play the following functions:

- To get attention or connect with others
- To avoid improving themselves or taking action
- To excuse your own poor performance
- To impress other people with your superiority or observational skill
- To incite others to break or form alliances
- To build support and power.

Complaining avoids accountability and distorts communication. Imagine the difference if people would bring you solutions instead of complaints. Jon Gordon in his book, "The No Complaint Rule" advises the use of three tools:

- The "but to positive". For example, I don't like my dinner but I am lucky to have food on the table.
- The "get to" instead of "have to". Like, changing *I have to go to work every day* to *I get to go to work every day so I can live my life*.
- Turn complaints into solutions; focus on solutions.

People tire of chronic complainers; people to whom complaining and negativity has become a habit. When they speak, others around them begin to "tune out." They know what's coming and they assume it's not constructive.

So far, this chapter has described some general considerations about communication and conversation. But managers and leaders have some specific responsibilities in this area. There needs to be a lot of conversation around the mission of the organization and its activities. Supervisors need to be continually reminding their staff about the connection of the work that they do with the mission of the organization. This should be a frequent message for two reasons. First is that as employees go about their daily tasks, they can easily lose focus, and so reminding them about the mission brings them back to the priorities and purpose of their work. Secondly, everyone is bombarded with messages these days, and it is only the ones that we hear the most frequently that will remain upper most in our minds. Advertisers used to say that the consumer had to hear a message 7 times before there was a chance that the ad would influence purchasing behavior. Now, we may need to hear a message 30 times before it will make a difference; the airwaves of life are just too crowded.

Supervisors and managers often complain that their staff fail to do what they are told; "they never listen to me.". There could be multiple problems here but remember that part of your responsibility is to teach people and how to things. And how does this learning take place? People have different learning styles: some learn by listening; others by observing; others learn a new procedure by actually doing it...interacting with it. As supervisor, if you wish to effectively communicate you will need to tailor your presentation style to the learning style of those you are talking to. Remember however that studies have shown that when it comes to someone's ability to retain information that *the more they can hear, see, discuss **and** use new information,* the more likely they will be to retain the information. So, if you want to make sure that your employees really understand a new procedure and will use it consistently, even when you are not around, give them the opportunity to learn the new procedure through as many different senses as possible.

Conversation that results in true communication is a wonderful tool to build positive relationships with people. If you are a supervisor or manager and want to gain the respect and admiration of your employees, simply talk with them. Hold conversations which are important to you and them. By doing this you acknowledge and honor the other person as an individual with inherent worth. In our electronic age where so much contact is digital and not face to face, your decision to take the time to talk to people will make you a special person amongst your colleagues.

Some of the most effective communication will occur informally...at the coffee pot, in the hallway, at lunch, maybe after work. These might be times when everyone is more relaxed and able to communicate more effectively. As a manager, use these times to further everyone's commitment to the agency mission and to build your personal relationship with your employees. To help this actually happen, put yourself on a quota of having at least three of these informal conversations each week. This will be nourishing for both you and the person you talk with. Don't forget to do it.

For Discussion

1. When was the last time you spent 15 minutes in conversation with a co-worker? Not about a problem or an issue, just in an attempt to understand them better.
2. Have you had a conversation with any of your direct reports about the mission of the organization? Make it a goal to have at least three of these conversations every week.
3. How do you respond to negative people and their complaints?
4. Demonstrate how non-verbal behavior can contradict what someone says verbally.
5. What non-verbal behaviors do you think are effective, when listening?
6. What are the steps you take to make sure that your staff understand a new procedure?

NOTES

nineteen

Manage Conflict

**"Peace is not absence of conflict; it is the ability
to handle conflict by peaceful means."
-Ronald Reagan**

Just what is conflict? It is basically a disagreement in which the people involved perceive a threat to their needs, interests or concerns. There is either the perception or the reality that needs are being denied by one party or the other. There can be a big difference however, between what is perceived and what is actually happening.

A recent article described how workplace conflict can ruin the best business plan. Some conflicts, the article said, are hot, full of hurt feelings and verbal sparring. However, and this I have found to be true, most workplace conflict is cold. Disagreement, although deep and long-standing, is held close to the vest and quietly acted out rather than discussed openly. Mistrust is present and spreads via whispers to third parties and is rarely confronted face-to-face.

Most people dislike conflict; it gives them a headache, upset stomach, ulcer, or worse. Recent study by organizational performance consultants indicated that 95% of employees have a

hard time confronting conflict and as a result substantial organization resources are wasted in a variety of conflict avoidance
tactics.

Generally people react to conflict in one of three ways: **passively, assertively or aggressively**. If you respond passively you allow
difficult people to dominate you. If this is you, probably you tend
to internalize discomfort with the situation. On the other hand, if
you respond aggressively, you tend to be very competitive and you
are determined to win all conflict at any cost. Assertive people on
the other hand are often able to negotiate a win-win resolution.
They are keenly aware of their own interests and needs and will
continue to work on the problem until a resolution is reached
which meets the needs of all parties. Each of these categories of
response has its particular advantages or disadvantages.

Within the three categories of conflict response described
above, there is a set of behaviors consistent with that response
mode. For example:

- Avoidance – we stay away from people, places and things
  which might include conflict themes.
- Accommodation – we don't change our mind but we
  manage to find a way to allow the other person to prevail.
- Competition – it's a matter of winning or losing, and
  being prepared to argue.
- Compromise – we are prepared to yield some of our views
  for the sake of a larger principle which survives. Each person "gives in" a little and either both parties are happy
  with the outcome, or as others have pointed out, no one
  is happy.
- Collaboration – this is a true win-win outcome. In this
  case, the conflicting parties may enter into long discussions so that both agree on the real principle at stake.

When we accomplish this, we are often able to agree on how to realize and accomplish our common goals and interests.

Interestingly enough, our own particular style of responding to conflict may have roots in our childhood. We learned how to deal with conflict by the example set in our own families.

How were conflicts resolved in your family? Often one parent or the other was the primary decision maker and nobody else really had an opportunity to learn and practice conflict resolution skills. In other families there was lots of shouting and hollering on the way to conflict resolution and everyone got into the act. In this latter scenario, a resolution may emerge from what might appear to be chaos.

But what about conflict in the workplace? It is frequently accompanied with a lack of understanding and a breach of good faith and trust, and co-workers can struggle with keeping the conflict or disagreement focused on the ideas or issues and not on people. In the workplace in particular, people often find themselves supporting a position which is good for them personally, or for their department. The same position may or may not be good for the organization. This dynamic of course can introduce a tone of emotion and defensiveness into the discussion.

Successful groups and teams however, have established ground rules about how conflict is dealt with and expressed. For example:

- It is acceptable to raise your voice
- It is not acceptable to use inappropriate language to express your feelings

- Group members cannot be attacked personally
- There will be a time limit on all debate and if an agreement is not reached, the matter will be tabled until the next meeting so that additional information and viewpoints can be gathered
- The conflict must stay focused on ideas and strategies and not focused on people

Group members, and especially the leader, must ensure that these ground rules are enforced and when necessary, modified.

Conflict can play a very important role in group decision-making however. It serves to clarify the issue by forcing both sides of the discussion to look more carefully at their position. Conflict uncovers new ideas, expands the creativity of group members and often leads to the best possible decision for the organization, a possibility that may or may not have been under review initially. Most organizations could benefit from more conflict, assuming that it is managed properly.

It helps if ideas are argued with a certain degree of emotion. When that happens, we know that the individual who is expressing the idea is expressing how he/she truly feels. When ideas are expressed only in intellectual terms, the true feelings of the individual may remain unclear. In order to arrive at the best decision, we need the true opinions of everyone present. Since we are all different, it stands to reason that we will view situations differently; we'll have different solutions to problems. If team members are all viewing a situation the same way, and have the same conclusions and recommendations, chances are someone is not being honest and there may even be a lack of trust present within the team.

Regardless of our own personal conflict approach style, several ideas may be helpful in dealing with workplace conflict. These tools encourage communication so that everyone feels safe to share their opinion, even if it is in the minority. If resolving a conflict has fallen into your area of responsibility, here are things you can do to accomplish the task and emerge with a workgroup with even stronger ties to each other:

1. Accept the fact that conflict makes people uncomfortable and that feeling may be present at one or more times in the process. Encourage team members to become accustomed to their feelings of discomfort; to not fight off the discomfort but see it as a normal part of the process of reaching the best solution. If you are a conflict avoider, you will find this a particularly difficult accomplishment.
2. Recognize that conflict may be necessary for productive results; if there is a lot of agreement but it seems "artificial", mine for conflict; push the discussion for areas of disagreement. This mining for conflict function can be led by the group leader or any other group member.
3. Give everyone a chance to voice an opinion and ask for clarification as needed. Generally people do not insist on having their own way, they just want to know that their opinion has been heard and seriously considered.
4. Be open-minded about possible solutions. Don't be limited to the solutions that have been used in the past and accept the fact that a new solution may require some fine-tuning – it may not seem initially like a good solution.
5. Establish and enforce clear ground rules for the debate. For example, keep the focus on issues and not on personalities. Other suggested ground rules are listed earlier in this chapter.

How conflict is handled can become deeply engrained in an organization's culture. Too often conflict is avoided, resulting in lots of unresolved issues which float through the organization and sap everyone's energy. The good news is that managing conflict, like lots of other leadership skills, can be improved.

Sometimes all it takes is a leader who is not afraid to speak the truth about things and at the same time can concretely demonstrate respect for the views of others. This encourages others to climb on board with the new cultural value of trust and honesty. Remember this quote from Patrick Lencioni, "Good conflict is about unfiltered, passionate debate around issues."

For Discussion

1. How was disagreement and conflict handled in your family of origin? Give examples. How has that experience influenced how you handle conflict today?
2. Being able to disagree requires honesty and trust. Does your workgroup trust each other? Are you able to be honest about how you truly feel or do you find yourself selecting your words very carefully based on who else is in the room?
3. What could be done in your organization to help work groups trust each other more?
4. Can you think of a time when an argument led to a really good problem resolution?
5. What happens when disagreements are ignored?

NOTES

twenty

Train, Train, Train

"The road to wisdom?-Well, it's plain and simple to express:
Err
and err
and err again
but less
and less
and less."
- Piet Hein, Danish inventor and poet

These are certainly tough times to be running an organization of any kind. Chances are regardless of your business, financial pressures have taken a toll. And the future is anything but clear. That's the new normal, as uncomfortable as it may seem. Many leaders are really good budget-balancers but thinking long term and understanding a strategy to continue to grow, even in tough economic times, is a taller order, but an important one nonetheless. Why is it that even in tough economic times, some organizations continue to grow while others go into hibernation?

Too often, when budgets are tight, staff training is one of the first things to be eliminated. Actually, when budgets are tight, staff training is more important than ever; it's a time when staff members need to strive for excellent performance. There is less room for uncertainty and incompetence. In this cost-cutting environment, eliminating staff training might actually make the organization less efficient. Here are examples of how staff training can save money through efficiency and effectiveness.

1. Training makes the good, better. All-star athletes train daily to keep their bodies in the peak of condition. They are always looking for a competitive edge; one hundredth of a second, one point, or one pitch can mean the difference between being a winner and an also-ran. Here in the beginning of the 21st century, there is competition even amongst non-profits. We should anticipate that a dwindling supply of public money will go to organizations that demonstrate success.

2. You can do more with less. What better time is there to make sure that employees are learning new skills? Depending on your business, better trained employees might mean fewer employees or lower levels of supervision.

3. Training benefits everyone…staff and clients. It's one way that the organization's commitment to success is expressed; where everyone strives to do a better job today than they did yesterday. It builds accountability into your organization. It results in better, more humane and more effective services for your clients, those you are trying to serve. In the for-profit world, studies have repeatedly demonstrated a direct relationship between the investment in employee training and the financial performance of the company.

4. More than any other single thing you can do, staff training encourages staff retention. Hopefully, many staff work for more than just a paycheck. They are looking for a connection with your organization's mission and the other employees who work there. They are looking to make an impact, to make a difference to those you serve. When they start to feel a lack of accomplishment that is when

they will start to leave you, regardless of how much money you are paying them. The last thing your clients need is a revolving door of staff coming in, and shortly thereafter, leaving. Training makes everyone more effective. Organize training which keeps people sharp; reminds them of their priorities and expands the number of tools they have available.

5. Though staff training might cost money it is less costly than turnover. In my own analysis with non-profit organizations, I have concluded that the out-of-pocket direct cost of staff turnover is approximately $1000 per incident. There are many indirect costs however which could easily drive the total cost to two to three times the direct cost figure. So, all by itself, reducing turnover can pay for a lot of training.

6. Training develops "bench strength." If you have done a good job of staff training and development, it will save you thousands of dollars in recruitment. Over the next 10 years, the majority of social service executives will reach the age of retirement. This drain of brain power and experience is strictly based on demographics, the result of having so many baby boomers in the workforce. Look at your group of middle managers and front line supervisors. Who there is ready for promotion? Interestingly nonprofits have a track record of going outside the agency to fill senior level vacancies and, as the Casey Foundation pointed out, that fact alone makes some effective middle managers hesitant about the next move up the ladder. So a social service agency will stand out in the crowd with an active staff development program and one that is backed up with an eagerness to fully utilize in-house talent.

7. You become a learning organization. When everyone (very top to very bottom) in the organization is involved in learning, it opens the door to a process of administrative and clinical improvement. Suddenly you become

better at problem solving and at identifying avenues for improvement.

8. You are seen as an employer of choice. The more active your organization is in training, the easier and less expensive your recruitment effort becomes. You develop a community reputation that you are an organization committed to the growth and success of employees.

The literature is full of examples where staff training has more than paid for itself. So, as we go into the future, make sure you are hiring good people, and when you have done that, make staff training one of the management tools that will ensure your organization's efficiency and effectiveness. Develop that part of your organizational culture which says that, "we all can do better than we have been doing." You'll be amazed at the difference it can make. It may be the difference between thriving and merely surviving.

Don't train employees just to appear concerned about employees or because you think training is something you should be doing. Use training to accomplish organizational objectives and measure its effectiveness in doing just that. This means that you must have a clear understanding of the needs of your organization, and that all training must be tied to one of those areas where you need to improve in order to continue to grow and thrive.

For Discussion

1. What are the signs that your organization is committed to learning?
2. What was the most effective training program you have had in the last three years? What made it effective?
3. How does your organization determine training needs?
4. Is training at your organization for everyone or only for a part of the organization?
5. When employees are promoted to opportunities within the organization, what has the organization done to ensure that they are prepared for the additional responsibilities?

NOTES

Conclusion

I hope that this book stimulates a lot of productive discussion in your organization. I have shared with you the most powerful ideas that I have developed in my 40 year career as a human services leader and have blended in some of the recent, progressive thinking in human resource management and organizational effectiveness.

I started writing this to help you and your employees experience greater levels of growth and success. If this happens, you can expect higher levels of staff satisfaction and productivity in your organization. I believe that employee success is a larger factor in employee satisfaction than is compensation.

The 20 ingredients you have just read about are not expensive to implement. To suggest a range of expensive options in the current environment would have been foolhardy on my part. They do however, require your time, commitment and attention. You will need to accept the fact that you need to help your employees refuel and re-energize. As I have said, "they are not computers...they do not run at high speed, day in and day out." Unless you are committed to their care, they will fatigue and that is when your expenses will truly rise.

Finally, don't start a new initiative just to say that you are doing something. Aim to improve the organization in a specific way. Establish performance improvement goals in relation to each initiative. A word of caution however. It wasn't a bad idea, just because it didn't work the first time. Rarely will a new initiative work as well as you want it to on the first try. Measure for results, modify and keep trying.

Organizational Assessment

Employee Centered Management

Quality Points

(check all those items which are true for your organization)

1. _____ The performance of management is measured in part by the performance of the people they have hired.

2. _____ Everyone has a job description and it has been updated in the last 2 years.

3. _____ Supervisors give each direct report at least one compliment every week.

4. _____ Each supervisor has a performance improvement plan.

5. _____ In addition to an orientation program, all new employees are assisted with their adjustment to the new job by a specified program of on-boarding.

6. _____ At least 70% of employees participate in an organization-wide staff satisfaction survey.

7. _____ The numbers of new hires leaving, for any reason, within 12 months of hire is decreasing.

8. _____ Supervisors leave at the designated end of shift at least 80% of the time.

9. _____ Within the last two weeks, there was a planned staff activity designed to be "fun".

10. _____ When an employee is involved in something that turns out badly, there is an effort to understand what really went wrong,

rather than asking the employee to shoulder all the blame prior to a review.

11. _____ Each employee has at least one colleague with whom they are able to share personal information.

12. _____ Employees are familiar with the financial condition of the organization?

13. _____ There is a plan to routinely communicate significant changes about the management of the organization to all employees

14. _____ Senior management frequently solicits suggestions from employees regarding the future of the organization.

15. _____ All employees receive at least one hour of 1:1 supervision each month.

16. _____ Successful supervisors are seen as those who support employees.

17. _____ Employees are encouraged to be creative problem solvers.

18. _____ Employees are encouraged to meet obligations to their families.

19. _____ All employees have attended at least two days of training within the last year.

20. _____ A completely confidential employee counseling program is available for all employees.

21. _____ Employees are given incentives to practice healthy life styles.

22. _____ There is at least one employee with expertise in "root cause analysis".

23. _____ Telling the truth is encouraged and reinforced…even when the truth is bad news.

24. _____ Supervisors discuss the mission of the organization with direct reports at least once each week.

25. _____ Rumors and office politics are seen as destructive and actively discouraged.

Scoring:

- 6 checks or less, you should prioritize the ones that are not checked and begin right away to address those as areas for improvement. It is very likely that your organization is suffering from a lack of success with clients as well as unhappy staff.
- 7-15 checks. You are probably no better or worse than most organizations but you could really gain a competitive advantage by addressing areas which seem problematic. If you are improving from a lower score that you had the last time, congratulations! Review the priority areas again, make sure they are still valid and move on to the next performance improvement area.
- 16-25 checks. Congratulations! Your organization is doing very well, but don't rest on your laurels. Most of the achievements you have realized require continual monitoring and maintenance. It's a great time for a Quality Improvement Committee to ensure you stay on the right track.

Research Notes

In order to make the entire book more readable, all references are aggregated in this section. It is intentionally not formatted according to customary literary guidelines. All sources used in this book however are easily found with the aid of any major internet search engine. It is my hope that these notes can be viewed by the reader as being more than just a list of sources that I used in preparing this book. Indeed what you have here is a library of resources you can use, above and beyond the content of this book, to examine and set your own workplace culture strategy.

Introduction
The quote from Jeff Haden is from the August, 2013 edition of *Inc.* magazine.

The 2013 Gallup Survey on Employee Engagement was released mid-year.

The Annie F. Casey Foundation's study of the social welfare workforce, released in 2006, highlighted the aging of organizational leadership in social services.

Omno Hamburger's forthcoming book has the working title of Happiness at Work.

Chapter 1
"Paying Attention to Turnover in the Non-Profit Sector" by Joe Brown on the Blog entitled <u>Mission Connected</u> 5/5/2010.

"How I Hire: The Must Haves; the Definitely Should Haves and The Game Changer" by Jack Welch. LinkedIn post 9/23/13.

Jack Welch operates the Jack Welch Management Institute. The web address is www.actnow.jwmi.com.

Carol Quinn's web site is www.hireauthority.com. At her web site you will find information about various workshops and web courses she offers on how to hire high performers. There are also links to a number of YouTube videos on the same subject.

Chapter 2
"How Companies Manage the Front Line Today" McKinsey Survey Results. February, 2010.

"Managers and Supervisors: Neglected Allies..." Change Management Learning Cener
"The Five Roles of a Supervisor. University Human Resources. University of Virginia.

Chapter 3
"Good Stats for Defending Training and Development Investment." Ron Thomas.
<u>Success Television.</u> April 25, 2011.

"The Ten Commandments of Employee On-Boarding: Career-Builder.com

Chapter 4
"Successful Delegation Prevents Turnover at Non-Profits." By Jana S. Ferris, Washington State University. December 27, 2010.
<u>Articles Base</u>

Chapter 5
"Experiential Happiness May be More Important than a Raise." By Manhattan Center Productions. October 22, 2013. The Sacremento Bee

"5 Fresh Trends to Fuse Fun and Work." By Meghan Biro. October 20, 2013. Talent Culture Consulting Group.

Alexander Kierulf, Chief Happiness Officer at TEDx Copenhagen. December 16, 2010 YouTube.com.

Delivering Happiness, A Path to Profits, Passion and Purpose. By Tony Hsieh. 2010

Chapter 6
The quote from Thomas Edison as well as references to high risk work settings are taken from an article in Psychology Today published on July 4, 2011 and written by Neil Farber, M.D., Ph.D. The title of the article is "The Organizational Blame Game."

"Welcome to the Church of Fail" by Leigh Buchanan, Inc. November, 2013

Chapter 7
"Study Reveals Employees' Lack of Trust in Managers." Today's Admin 2010

The Advantage, by Patrick Lencioni. 2012

"What to do When Trust with Your Employees Breaks Down" by Vanessa Hall. February 28, 2011. TLNT Webinars.

How to Build Trust in an Organization by Chris Hitch, Ph.D. University of North Carolina Kenan-Flagler Business School. 2012.

Chapter 8
"5 Tips for Employers to Earn Respect from Employees." By Lisa Quast. <u>Forbes</u> September, 2012.

"Respecting Your Employees is Good Business." By Melinda Guillemette. 2009

"Respect" – Aretha Franklin, Original Version, 1967. Atlantic Records

Author and Philosopher Charles R. Swindoll

Chapter 9
"Job Security, Company Stability are Most Important, Generations Agree" by Kathy Gurchiek. Society of Human Resource Management. July 12, 2010.

"Job Security Makes for Better Workers" by Cheung Wing Kwan. April 14, 2003.
<u>South China Morning Post.</u>

"A Better Way of Conducting Layoffs". By Darren Dahl. <u>Inc.</u> July 19, 2011

Chapter 10
"The Power of Touch: How Physical Contact Can Improve Your Health" by Diana Spechler. <u>Huffington Post</u> May 14, 2013

"Lifelong Effects of Early Childhood Adversity and Toxic Stress" by Drs. John Shonkoff and Andrew Garner. September, 2011. <u>Pediatrics: The Official Journal of the American Academy of Pediatrics.</u>

<u>Family Caregiver Alliance,</u> www.caregiver.org. "Fact Sheet and Publications"

"Community Supports" www.easyaccess.virginia.gov/caregiver-support

Chapter 11
The quote from Martin Luther King, Jr. was taken from a video produced by motivational speaker and Conductor of the Boston Philharmonic, Benjamin Zander.
The Art of Possibility video. Enterprise Media.com. 2006.

The rules for brainstorming as articulated by Alex Osborn are described at the website www.CreativityTraining.com

Chapter 12
Kevin Kruse is a best selling author and I have quoted from his book, published in 2011 entitled, **We, How to Increase Performance and Profits through Full Engagement.** By Kevin Kruse and Rudy Karsan.

"I Can't Get no Satisfaction" by John Gibbons, published in 2010 as part of the Conference Board Report.

Chapter 13
"Cost-Benefit Analysis of Employee Recognition" Cutting Edge PR. July, 2013

"5 Ways Leaders Rock Employee Recognition" by Meghan Biro. Forbes January, 2013

Chapter 14
The reference to system failure is borrowed from the writing of management consultant W. Edwards Deming as reported in a white paper on Accountability prepared by the consulting firm PP&S in 2010.

The reference to the negative relationship which often exists between employees and supervisors is taken from a 2010 study performed by researchers at the University of Florida – "The Seven Deadly Sins of Workplace Managers."

HBR Blog Network. "Four Tips for Building Accountability" by Rosabeth Moss Kanter. August 19, 2009.

Chapter 15

Wikipedia defines compassion fatigue, also known as **secondary traumatic stress** (STS), as a condition characterized by a gradual lessening of compassion over time. It is common among individuals that work directly with trauma victims such as nurses, psychologists, and first responders.

An article in Forbes magazine for June 11, 2013 established a link between employee wellness and the bottom line financial performance of a company.

S. Bloom and B. Faragher. Restoring Sanctuary: A New Operating System for Trauma-Informed Organizations. 2013. New York. Oxford University Press.

Chapter 16

Some material in this chapter is taken from one or more of the following sources:
- Death by Meeting - by Patrick Lencioni, a well-known author and speaker on subjects having to do with organizational performance and team building.
- "Managing Difficult Meeting Participants" – blog post by Linda L. Mather of Beacon Consulting Associates of Princeton, NJ.
- "Meeting De-Railers: How to Manage Difficult Participants" Blog post of 1/27/13 by leadservs.com.

Patrick Lencioni. <u>The Advantage: Why Organizational Health Trumps Everything Else in Business.</u> 2012. New York. Jossey-Boss.

Chapter 17
American comedian George Carlin first discussed his "seven dirty words you can't say on TV" monologue in 1972.

<u>Forget it For Success: Walking Away from Outdated, Counterproductive Beliefs</u> by Eric Harvey and Steve Ventura. 1997. Dallas, Texas. Performance Publishing.

Chapter 18
<u>The No-Complaining Rule: Positive Ways to Deal with Negativity at Work.</u> By Jon Gordon. 2008. Wiley.

"13 Simple Ways You Can Have More Meaningful Conversations" by John Hall.
<u>Forbes</u> August 18, 2013.

"What is the Rule of 7?" Baby Boomer Entrepreneur, Andrea Stenberg. 10/17/09

www.willatworklearning.com

Chapter 19
Joseph Grenny in <u>Talent Management</u> magazine, September 2012

You Tube Video on how employees respond to conflict uploaded by VitalSmarts on 2/24/12.

Patrick Lencioni discusses how conflict can benefit an organization in his book, <u>The Advantage</u>, published in 2012. (See reference note for Chap. 16)

Chapter 20

For a data-rich review of the issues discussed in this chapter, see The Relationship Between Training and Business Performance. Cosh, Hughes, Bullock, Putton. University of Cambridge Press. July 2003.

Acknowledgements

This is not just my book; there are many people who have played an important role in completing this project.

First of all there is Diane and Kristi, my wife and teenaged daughter, who by this time have gotten accustomed to my hours on the computer but whose patience I nonetheless appreciate.

Secondly several individuals made unique and special contributions. This book would not have been possible without the continuous support of Douglas McCown. Douglas McGruther contributed his editorial services. Jan Pavis-Sparks, supplemented the opinion of many readers of my newsletter, The Mentor, with a title suggestion that really struck a useful chord for me. Annie Lachs and I worked together for many years and she helped me formulate many concepts that made their way into this book. And finally, my sister-in-law, Karen Wenger, served as the word processor for this project.

At each organization where I have been employed over the years, there have been people who helped me learn and grow. These are the people who taught me about management and so they also have had a role in this book. I didn't always heed their advice but their ideas were helpful nonetheless. I have maintained relationships with some of these people over the years and their support and encouragement is always a source of inspiration. In particular:, Jackie Lowe, Benjamin Spedding, Jim

Harnett, Lonnie Phillips and the many valued colleagues in the Teaching Family Association.

Last but not least, I wish to express my thanks to William Waldman, Executive-in-Residence at the Rutgers University School of Social Work for his willingness to review this manuscript and prepare the Forward. Thanks Bill!

Larry Wenger, MSW

Information on Multiple Copies of This Book and Speaking Engagements

This book is really meant to be read and discussed in a staff group. If you would like to order multiple copies of this book or if you would like to invite Larry Wenger to speak with your staff group, please call:

1-877-872-6195

or contact by email at:

lwenger@workforceperformancegroup.net

or by surface mail:

Larry Wenger
Workforce Performance Group
821 Dolington Rd.
Newtown, Pa. 18940

Made in the USA
Charleston, SC
01 October 2014